The

Compleat Angler;

or the

Contemplative Man's Recreation.

Being a Discourse

of

FISH and FISHING,

Not unworthy the perusal of most

Anglers.

BY IZAAK WALTON.

Simon Peter *said, I go a* fishing : *and they said,
We also wil go with thee.* John xxi. 3.

London, Printed by *T. Maxey* for RICH. MARRIOT, in
S Dunstans Church-yard, Fleet street, 1653.

LONDON:
ALEX. MURRAY AND SON, 30, QUEEN'S SQUARE, W.C.

1869.

189. g. 64.

MURRAY'S REPRINTS.

THE COMPLEAT ANGLER,

BY

IZAAK WALTON,

EDITION 1653,

Forms the second of this series; and, retaining the quaint originality of the unique work, has been carefully gone over by

A. MURRAY.

May 20th, 1869.

To the Right Worshipful

JOHN OFFLEY

Of MADELY Manor in the County of *Stafford*, Esq.,

My most honoured Friend.

SIR,

*I have made so ill use of your former favors, as by
them to be encouraged to intreat that they may be enlarged
to the* patronage *and* protection *of this Book; and I have
put on a modest confidence, that I shall not be denyed,
because 'tis a discourse of* Fish *and* Fishing, *which you
both know so well, and love and practice so much.*

*You are assur'd (though there be ignorant men of an
other belief) that* Angling *is an Art; and you know that
art better than any that I know: and that this is truth, is
demonstrated by the fruits of that pleasant labor which
you enjoy when you purpose to give rest to your mind,
and devest your self of your more serious business, and
(which is often) dedicate a day or two to this* Recreation.

*At which time, if common Anglers should attend you,
and be eye-witnesses of the success, not of your fortune,
but your skill, it would doubtless beget in them an emulation to be like you, and that emulation might beget an industrious diligence to be so: but I know it is not atainable
by common capacities.*

*Sir, this pleasant curiositie of Fish and Fishing (of
wch you are so great a master) has been thought worthy the*
pens *and* practices *of divers in other nations, which have
been reputed men of great* Learning *and* Wisdome; *and
amongst those of this nation, I remember* Sir Henry
Wotton *(a dear lover of this art) has told me, that his
intentions were to write a discourse of the art, and in the*

praise of Angling, *and doubtless he had done so, if death had not prevented him; the remembrance of which hath often made me sorry; for, if he had lived to do it, then the unlearned* Angler *(of which I am one) had seen some treatise of this art worthy his perusal, which (though some have undertaken it) I could never yet see in English.*

But mine may be thought as weak *and as* unworthy *of common view: and I do here freely confess, that I should rather excuse my self, than censure others, my own discourse being liable to so many exceptions; against which, you (Sir) might make this one.* That it can contribute nothing to your knowledge; *and lest a longer epistle may diminish your pleasure, I shal not adventure to make this epistle longer than to add this following truth,* that I am really, Sir,

Your most affectionate Friend,

and most humble Servant,

IZ. WA.

TO THE

Reader of this Discourse:

But especially

To the honest ANGLER.

I think fit to tell thee these following truths; that I did not undertake to write, or to publish this discourse of *fish* and *fishing*, to please my self, and that I wish it may not displease others; for, I have confest there are many defects in it. And yet, I cannot doubt, but that by it, some readers may receive so much *profit* or *pleasure*, as if they be not very busie men, may make it not unworthy the time of their perusall; and this is all the confidence that I can put on concerning the merit of this book.

And I wish the reader also to take notice, that in writing of it, I have made a recreation, of a recreation; and that it might prove so to thee in the reading, and not to read *dull* and *tediously*, I have in severall places mixt some innocent mirth; of which, if thou be a severe, sowr complexioned man, then I here disallow thee to be a competent judge. For divines say, *there are offences given;* and *offences taken, but not given.* And I am the willinger to justifie this *innocent mirth*, because the whole discourse is a kind of picture of my owne disposition, at least of my disposition in such daies and times as I allow my self, when honest *Nat.* and *R. R.* and I go a fishing together.

And I am also to tel the reader, that in that which is the more usefull part of this discourse; that is to say, the observations of the *nature* and *breeding*, and *seasons*, and *catching of fish*, I am not so simple as not to think but that he may find exceptions in some of these; and therefore I must intreat him to know, or rather note, that severall countreys, and several rivers alter the *time* and *manner* of fishes breeding; and therefore if he bring not candor to the reading of this discourse, he shall both injure me, and possibly himself too by too many criticisms.

Now for the art of catching fish; that is to say, how to make a man that was none, an Angler by a book: he that undertakes it, shall undertake a harder task than *Hales*, that in his printed book* undertook by it to teach the art of fencing, and was laught at for his labour. Not but that something usefull might be observed out of that book; but that art was not to be taught by words; nor is the art of angling. And yet, I think, that most that love that game, may here learn something that may be worth their money, if they be not needy: and if they be, then my advice is, that they forbear; for, I write not to get money, but for pleasure; and this discourse boasts of no more: for I hate to promise much, and fail.

But pleasure I have found both in the *search* and *conference* about what is here offered to thy view and censure; I wish thee as much in the perusal of it, and so might here take my leave; but I will stay thee a little longer by telling thee, that whereas it is said by many, that in *Fly-fishing* for a *Trout*, the angler must observe

* Called the Private School of Defence.

his twelve flyes for every month, I say, if he observe that, he shall be as certain to catch fish, as they that make hay by the fair dayes in almanacks, and be no surer: for doubtless, three or four *Flyes* rightly made, do serve for a *Trout* all *summer;* and for *winter-flies,* all *anglers* know, they are as useful as an *almanack* out of date.

Of these (because no man is born an *artist* nor an *angler*) I thought fit to give thee this notice. I might say more, but it is not fit for this place; but if this discourse which follows shall come to a second impression, which is possible, for slight books have been in this age observed to have that fortune; I shall then for thy sake be glad to correct what is faulty, or by a conference with any to explain or enlarge what is defective: but for this time I have neither a willingness nor leasure to say more, than wish thee a *rainy evening* to read this book in, and *that the east wind may never blow when thou goest a fishing.* Farewel.

Iz. Wa.

BECAUSE in this discourse of *Fish* and *Fishing* I have not observed a method, which (though the discourse be not long) may be some inconvenience to the reader, I have therefore for his easier finding out some particular things which are spoken of, made this following table.

In chap. 6. *are some observations concerning the* Salmon, *with direction how to* fish *for him.*

In chap. 7. *are several observations concerning the* Luce *or* Pike, *with some directions how and with what baits to fish for him.*

In chap. 8. *are several observations of the nature and breeding of* Carps, *with some observations how to* angle *for them.*

In chap. 9. *are some observations concerning the* Bream, *the* Tench, *and* Pearch, *with some directions with what baits to* fish *for them.*

In chap. 10. *are several observations of the* nature *and* breeding of Eeles, *with advice how to fish for them.*

In chap. 11. *are some observations of the nature and breeding of* Barbels, *with some advice how, and with what baits to fish for them ; as also for the* Gudgion *and* Bleak.

In chap. 12. *are general directions how and with what baits to fish for the* Ruffe *or* Pope, *the* Roch, *the* Dace, *and other smal fish, with directions how to keep* Ant-flies *and* Gentles *in winter, with some observations not unfit to be known of* Anglers.

In chap. 13. *are observations for the colouring of your* Rod *and* Hair.

These directions the reader may take as an ease in his search after some particular fish, and the baits proper for them ; and he will shew himselfe courteous in mending or passing by some errors in the printer, which are not so many but that they may be pardoned.

COMPLEAT ANGLER,

OR THE

CONTEMPLATIVE MAN'S RECREATION.

PISCATOR.—VIATOR.

Piscator.

YOU are wel overtaken, sir ; a good morning to you ; I have stretch'd my legs up *Totnam Hil* to overtake you, hoping your businesse may occasion you towards *Ware*, this fine pleasant fresh *May day* in the morning.

Viator. Sir, I shall almost answer your hopes : for my purpose is to be at *Hodsden* (three miles short of that town) I wil not say, before I drink ; but before I break my fast : for I have appointed a friend or two to meet me there at the *Thatcht House*, about nine of the clock this morning ; and that made me so early up, and indeed, to walk so fast.

Pisc. Sir, I know the *Thatcht House* very well : I often make it my resting place, and taste a cup of ale there, for which liquor that place is very remarkable ; and to that house I shall by your favour accompany you, and either abate of my pace, or mend it, to enjoy such a companion as you seem to be, knowing that (as the Italians say) *good company makes the way seem shorter.*

Viat. It may do so, sir, with the help of good discourse, which (me thinks) I may promise from you, that both look and speak so chearfully. And to invite you to it, I do here promise you, that for my part, I will be as free and open-hearted, as discretion will warrant me to be with a stranger.

Pisc. Sir, I am right glad of your answer ; and in con-

fidence that you speak the truth, I shall (sir) put on a bold-
nesse to ask, whether pleasure or businesse has occasioned
your journey.

Viat. Indeed, sir, a little businesse and more pleasure ;
for my purpose is to bestow a day or two in hunting the
Otter (which my friend that I go to meet, tells me is more
pleasant than any hunting whatsoever :) and having dis-
patcht a little businesse this day, my purpose is to-morrow
to follow a pack of dogs of honest Mr. ——, who hath appointed me and my friend to meet him upon *Amwell Hill*
to-morrow morning by day break.

Pisc. Sir, my fortune hath answered my desires ; and
my purpose is to bestow a day or two in helping to destroy
some of those villainous vermin : for I hate them perfectly,
because they love fish so well, or rather because they destroy so much : indeed, so much, that in my judgment all
men that keep Otter dogs ought to have a pension from the
commonwealth to incourage them to destroy the very
breed of those base *Otters*, they do so much mischief.

Viat. But what say you to the *Foxes* of this nation ?
would not you as willingly have them destroyed ? for
doubtlesse they do as much mischief as the *Otters*.

Pisc. Oh Sir, if they do, it is not so much to me and
my fraternitie, as that base vermin the *Otters* do.

Viat. Why sir, I pray, of what fraternity are you, that
you are so angry with the poor *Otter ?*

Pisc. I am a brother of the *Angle*, and therefore an
enemy to the *Otter*, he does me and my friends so much
mischief, for you are to know, that we *Anglers* all love
one another : and therefore do I hate the *Otter* perfectly,
even for their sakes that are of my brotherhood.

Viat. Sir, to be plain with you, I am sorry you are an
Angler : for I have heard many grave, serious men pitie,
and many pleasant men scoffe at *Anglers*.

Pisc. Sir, There are many men that are by others
taken to be serious grave men, which we contemn and
pitie ; men of sowre complexions ; mony-getting-men, that
spend all their time first in getting, and next in anxious
care to keep it : men that are condemn'd to be rich, and
alwayes discontented, or busie. For these poor-rich-men,

wee Anglers pitie them ; and stand in no need to borrow
their thoughts to think our selves happie : For (trust me,
sir) we enjoy a contentednesse above the reach of such
dispositions.

And as for any scoffer, *qui mockat mockabitur.* Let
mee tell you, (that you may tell him) what the wittie
French-man sayes* in such a case. *When my* cat *and I
entertaine each other with mutuall apish tricks (as playing
with a garter,) who knows but that I make her more sport
then she makes me ? Shall I conclude her simple, that
has her time to begin or refuse sportivenesse as freely as I
my self have ? Nay, who knows but that our agreeing no
better, is the defect of my not understanding her language ?
(for doubtlesse cats talk and reason with one another) and
that shee laughs at, and censures my folly, for making her
sport, and pities mee for understanding her no better ?* To
this purpose speaks *Mountagne* concerning *Cats :* And I
hope I may take as great a libertie to blame any scoffer,
that has never heard what an angler can say in the justification of his art and pleasure.

But, if this satisfie not, I pray bid the scoffer put this
epigram into his pocket, and read it every morning for his
breakfast (for I wish him no better ;) hee shall finde it
fix'd before the dialogues of *Lucian* (who may be justly
accounted the father of the family of all *scoffers :*) and
though I owe none of the fraternitie so much as good will,
yet I have taken a little pleasant pains to make such a
conversion of it as may make it the fitter for all of that
fraternity.

> *Lucian* well skill'd in *scoffing*, this has writ,
> Friend, that's your folly which you think your wit :
> This you vent oft, void both of *wit* and *fear*,
> Meaning an other, when your self you jeer.

But no more of the *scoffer ;* for since *Solomon** sayes,
he is an abomination to men, he shall be so to me ; and I
think, to all that love *Vertue* and *Angling.*

Viat. Sir, you have almost amazed me : for though I

---

* The Lord Mountagne in his Apol. for Ra. Sebond.   † Pro. 24. 9.

am no scoffer, yet I have (I pray let me speak it without offence) alwayes look'd upon *Anglers* as more patient, and more simple men, then (I fear) I shall finde you to be.

Pisc. Sir, I hope you will not judge my earnestness to be impatience : and for my *simplicitie*, if by that you mean a *harmlesnesse*, or that *simplicity* that was usually found in the primitive Christians, who were (as most *Anglers* are) quiet men, and followed peace ; men that were too wise to sell their consciences to buy riches for vexation, and a fear to die. Men that lived in those times when there were fewer lawyers ; for then a lordship might have been safely conveyed in a piece of parchment no bigger than your hand, though several skins are not sufficient to do it in this wiser age. I say, sir, if you take us Anglers to be such simple men as I have spoken of, then both my self, and those of my profession will be glad to be so understood. But if by simplicitie you meant to expresse any general defect in the understanding of those that professe and practise *Angling*, I hope to make it appear to you, that there is so much contrary reason (if you have but the patience to hear it) as may remove all the anticipations that time or discourse may have possess'd you with, against that ancient and laudable art.

Viat. Why (sir) is angling of antiquitie, and an art, and an art not easily learn'd ?

Pisc. Yes (sir :) and I doubt not but that if you and I were to converse together but til night, I should leave you possess'd with the same happie thoughts that now possesse me ; not onely for the antiquitie of it, but that it deserves commendations ; and that 'tis an art ; and worthy the knowledge and practice of a wise, and a serious man.

Viat. Sir, I pray speak of them what you shall think fit ; for wee have yet five miles to walk before wee shall come to the *Thatcht house.* And, sir, though my infirmities are many, yet I dare promise you, that both my patience and attention will indure to hear what you will say till wee come thither : and if you please to begin in order with the antiquity, when that is done, you shall not want my attention to the commendations and accommodations of it : and lastly, if you shall convince me that 'tis an art, and an art worth learning, I shall beg I may become your scholer, both to wait upon you, and to be instructed in the art it self.

Pisc. Oh sir, 'tis not to be questioned, but that it is an art, and an art worth your learning; the question wil rather be, whether you be capable of learning it? For he that learns it, must not onely bring an enquiring, searching, and discerning wit; but he must bring also that *patience* you talk of, and a love and propensity to the art it self: but having once got and practised it, then doubt not but the art will (both for the pleasure and profit of it) prove like to *vertue, a reward to it self.*

Viat. Sir, I am now become so ful of expectation, that I long much to have you proceed in your discourse: And first, I pray sir, let me hear concerning the antiquity of it.

Pisc. Sir, I wil preface no longer, but proceed in order as you desire me : and first for the antiquity of *Angling,* I shall not say much; but onely this; some say, it is as ancient as *Deucalions* floud *; and others (which I like better) say, that *Belus*† (who was the inventor of godly and vertuous recreations) was the inventer of it: and some others say, (for former times have had their disquisitions about it) that *Seth,* one of the sons of *Adam,* taught it to his sons, and that by them it was derived to posterity. Others say, that he left it engraved on those pillars which hee erected to preserve the knowledg of the *mathematicks, musick,* and the rest of those precious arts, which by Gods appointment or allowance, and his noble industry were thereby preserved from perishing in *Noah's* floud.

These (my worthy friend) have been the opinions of some men, that possibly may have endeavoured to make it more ancient than may well be warranted. But for my part, I shall content my self in telling you, that *Angling* is much more ancient than the incarnation of our Saviour: for both in the prophet *Amos*‡, and before him in *Job*§, (which last book is judged to be written by *Moses*) mention is made of *fish-hooks,* which must imply *Anglers* in those times.

But (my worthy friend) as I would rather prove my self

* J. Da.   † Jer. Mar.   ‡ Chap. 4. 2.   § Chap. 41.

to be a gentleman, by being *learned* and *humble, valiant* and *inoffensive, vertuous* and *communicable,* then by a fond ostentation of *riches;* or (wanting these vertues my self) boast that these were in my ancestors; [And yet I confesse, that where a noble and ancient descent and such merits meet in any man, it is a double dignification of that person :] and so, if this antiquitie of Angling (which, for my part, I have not forc'd) shall, like an ancient familie, be either an honour, or an ornament to this vertuous art which I both love and practise, I shall be the gladder that I made an accidental mention of it ; and shall proceed to the justification, or rather commendation of it.

Viat. My worthy friend, I am much pleased with your discourse, for that you seem to be so ingenuous, and so modest, as not to stretch arguments into hyperbolicall expressions, but such as indeed they will reasonably bear ; and I pray, proceed to the justification, or commendations of Angling, which I also long to hear from you.

Pisc. Sir, I shall proceed ; and my next discourse shall be rather a commendation, than a justification of Angling : for, in my judgment, if it deserves to be commended, it is more than justified ; for some practices that may be justified, deserve no commendation : yet there are none that deserve commendation but may be justified.

And now having said this much by way of preparation, I am next to tell you, that in ancient times a debate hath risen, (and it is not yet resolved) whether *contemplation* or *action* be the chiefest thing wherein the happiness of a man doth most consist in this world?

Concerning which, some have maintained their opinion of the first, by saying, ["that the nearer we mortals come to God by way of imitation, the more happy we are :"] and that God injoyes himself only by *contemplation* of his own *goodness, eternity, infiniteness,* and *power,* and the like ; and upon this ground many of them prefer *contemplation* before *action :* and indeed, many of the fathers seem to approve this opinion, as may appear in their comments upon the words of our Saviour to * *Martha.*

And contrary to these, others of equal authority and

* Luk. 10. 41, 42.

credit, have preferred *action* to be chief; as experiments
in *Physick*, and the application of it, both for the ease and
prolongation of man's life, by which man is enabled to
act, and to do good to others: and they say also, that *action*
is not only doctrinal, but a maintainer of humane society;
and for these, and other reasons, to be preferr'd before
contemplation.

Concerning which two opinions, I shall forbear to add a
third, by declaring my own, and rest myself contented in
telling you (my worthy friend) that both these meet together, and do most properly belong to the most honest,
ingenious, harmless art of angling.

And first I shall tel you what some have observed, and
I have found in my self, that the very sitting by the river's
side, is not only the fittest place for, but will invite the
anglers to contemplation: that it is the fittest place, seems
to be witnessed by the children of *Israel;* * who, having
banish'd all mirth and musick from their pensive hearts,
and having hung up their then mute instruments upon the
willow trees, growing by the rivers of *Babylon*, sate down
upon those banks bemoaning the *ruines* of *Sion*, and con-
templating their own sad condition.

And an ingenuous *Spaniard* sayes, ["that both rivers,
and the inhabitants of the watery element, were created
for wise men to contemplate, and fools to pass by without
consideration."] And though I am too wise to rank my
self in the first number, yet give me leave to free my self
from the last, by offering to thee a short contemplation,
first of rivers, and then of fish: concerning which, I doubt
not but to relate to you many things very considerable.

Concerning rivers, there be divers wonders reported of
them by authors, of such credit, that we need not deny
them an historical faith.

As of a river in *Epirus*, that puts out any lighted torch,
and kindles any torch that was not lighted. Of the river
Selarus, that in a few hours turns a rod or a wand into
stone (and our *Camden* mentions the like wonder in *England:*) that there is a river in *Arabia*, of which all the
sheep that drink thereof have their wool turned into a ver-

* Psal. 137.

milion colour. And one of no less credit than *Aristotle,** tels us of a merry river, the river *Elusina*, that dances at the noise of musick, that with musick it bubbles, dances, and growes sandy, but returns to a wonted calmness and clearness when the musick ceases. And lastly, (for I would not tire your patience) *Josephus*, that learned *Jew*, tells us of a river in *Judea*, that runs and moves swiftly all the six dayes of the week, and stands still and rests upon their *Sabbath* day. But sir, lest this discourse may seem tedious, I shall give it a sweet conclusion out of that holy poet Mr. *George Herbert* his divine contemplation on God's providence.

Lord, who hath praise enough, nay, who hath any?
None can express thy works, but he that knows them;
And none can know thy works, they are so many,
And so complete, but only he that owes them.

We all acknowledge both thy power and love
To be exact, transcendent, and divine;
Who dost so strangely, and so sweetly move,
Whilst all things have their end, yet none but thine.

Wherefore, most sacred spirit, I here present
For me, and all my fellows, praise to thee;
And just it is that I should pay the rent,
Because the benefit accrues to me.

And as concerning fish, in that psalm,† wherein, for height of poetry and wonders, the prophet *David* seems even to exceed himself; how doth he there express him-selfe in choice metaphors, even to the amazement of a contemplative reader, concerning the sea, the rivers, and the fish therein contained. And the great naturallist *Pliny* sayes, ["that Nature's great and wonderful power is more demonstrated in the sea, than on the land."] And this may appear by the numerous and various creatures, in-habiting both in and about that element: as to the readers of *Gesner, Randelitius* ‡ *Pliny, Aristotle,* and others is

* In his *Wonders of Nature.* This is confirmed by *Ennius,* and *Solon* in his holy History.　　　† Psal. 104.　　　‡ [Rondelet.]

demonstrated : but I will sweeten this discourse also out
of a contemplation in divine *Dubartas*,* who sayes,

> God quickned in the sea and in the rivers,
> So many fishes of so many features,
> That in the waters we may see all creatures ;
> Even all that on the earth is to be found,
> As if the world were in deep waters drownd.
> For seas (as well as skies) have sun, moon, stars ;
> (As wel as air) swallows, rooks, and stares ;
> (As wel as earth) vines, roses, nettles, melons,
> Mushrooms, pinks, gilliflowers, and many milions
> Of other plants, more rare, more strange then these ;
> As very fishes living in the seas ;
> And also rams, calves, horses, hares and hogs,
> Wolves, urchins, lions, elephants and dogs ;
> Yea, men and maids, and which I most admire,
> The mitred bishop, and the cowled fryer.
> Of which examples but a few years since,
> Were shown the *Norway* and *Polonian* prince.

These seem to be wonders, but have had so many con-
firmations from men of learning and credit, that you need
not doubt them ; nor are the number, nor the various
shapes of fishes, more strange or more fit for *contemplation*,
than their different natures, inclinations and actions : concerning which I shall beg your patient ear a little longer.

The *cuttle-fish* wil cast a long gut out of her throat,
which (like as an angler does his line) she sendeth forth
and pulleth in again at her pleasure, according as she sees
some little fish come neer to her ; and the *cuttle-fish* †
(being then hid in the gravel) lets the smaller fish nibble
and bite the end of it ; at which time shee by little and
little draws the smaller fish so neer to her, that she may
leap upon her, and then catches and devours her : and for
this reason some have called this fish the *sea-angler*.

There are also lustful and chaste fishes, of which I shall
also give you examples.

And first, what *Dubartas* sayes of a fish called the

---

* *Dubartas* in the fifth day.   † *Mount. Essayes :* and others affirm this.

Sargus; which (because none can express it better than he does) I shall give you in his own words, supposing it shall not have the less credit for being verse, for he hath gathered this, and other observations, out of authors that have been great and industrious searchers into the secrets of nature.

> The adulterous *Sargus* doth not only change
> Wives every day in the deep streams, but (strange)
> As if the honey of sea-love delight
> Could not suffice his ranging appetite,
> Goes courting *she-goats* on the grassie shore,
> Horning their husbands that had horns before.

And the same author writes concerning the *Cantharus,* that which you shall also heare in his own words.

> But contrary, the constant *Cantharus,*
> Is ever constant to his faithful spouse,
> In nuptial duties spending his chaste life,
> Never loves any but his own dear wife.

Sir, but a little longer, and I have done.

Viat. Sir, take what liberty you think fit, for your discourse seems to be musick, and charms me into an attention.

Pisc. Why then, sir, I will take a little libertie to tell, or rather to remember you what is said of *turtle doves:* first, that they silently plight their troth and marry; and that then, the survivor scorns (as the *Thracian* women are said to do) to outlive his or her mate ; and this is taken for such a truth, that if the survivor shall ever couple with another, the he or she, not only the living, but the dead, is denied the *name* and *honour* of a true *turtle dove.*

And to parallel this land variety, and teach mankind moral faithfulness, and to condemn those that talk of religion, and yet come short of the moral faith of fish and fowl ; men that violate the law, affirm'd by saint *Paul* to to be writ in their hearts,* and which he sayes shal at the last day condemn and leave them without excuse. I pray hearken to what *Dubartas* sings :† (for the hearing of such

---

* Rom. 2. 14, 15. † *Dubartas* 5. day.

conjugal faithfulness, will be musick to all chaste ears)
and therefore, I say, hearken to what *Dubartas* sings of
the *Mullet :*

> But for chaste love the *Mullet* hath no peer,
> For, if the fisher hath surprised her pheer,
> As mad with wo, to shoare she followeth,
> Prest to consort him both in life and death.

On the contrary, what shall I say of the *house-cock,*
which treads any *hen,* and then, (contrary to the *swan,*
the *partridg,* and *pigeon*) takes no care to hatch, to feed,
or to cherish his own brood, but is senseless though they
perish.

And 'tis considerable, that the *hen* (which because she
also takes any *cock,* expects it not) who is sure the chickens
be her own, hath a moral impression her care, and affection to her own broode, more than doubled, even to such
a height, that our Saviour in expressing his love to *Jeru-
salem,** quotes her for an example of tender affection, as
his Father had done *Job* for a pattern of patience.

And to parallel this *cock,* there be divers fishes that cast
their spawne on flags or stones, and then leave it uncovered
and exposed to become a prey, and be devoured by vermine or other fishes (as namely the *Barbel*) take such care
for the preservation of their seed, that (unlike to the *cock*
or the *cuckoe*) they mutually labour (both the spawner and
the melter) to cover their spawne with sand, or watch it,
or hide it in some secret place unfrequented by vermine,
or by any fish but themselves.

Sir, these examples may, to you and others, seem
strange ; but they are testified, some by *Aristotle,* some
by *Pliny,* some by *Gesner,* and by divers others of credit,
and are believed and known by divers, both of wisdom
and experience, to be a truth ; and are (as I said at the
beginning) fit for the contemplation of a most serious, and
a most pious man.

And that they be fit for the contemplation of the most
prudent and pious, and peaceable men, seems to be
testified by the practice of so many devout and contem-

* Mat. 23. 37.

plative men ; as the patriarks or prophets of old, and of the apostles of our Saviour in these later times, of which twelve he chose four that were fishermen : concerning which choice some have made these observations.

First, That he never reproved these for their imployment or calling, as he did the scribes and the mony-changers. And secondly, that he found the hearts of such men, men that by nature were fitted for contemplation and quietness ; men of mild, and sweet, and peaceable spirits, as (indeed most anglers are) these men our blessed Saviour (who is observed to love to plant grace in good natures) though nothing be too hard for him, yet these men he chose to call from their irreprovable imployment, and gave them grace to be his disciples and to follow him.

And it is observable, that it was our Saviours will that his four fishermen apostles should have a prioritie of no-mination in the catalogue of his twelve apostles, as namely first, S. *Peter, Andrew, James* and *John,** and then the rest in their order.

And it is yet more observable, that when our blessed Saviour went up into the mount, at his transfiguration, when he left the rest of his disciples and chose onely three to bear him company, that these three were all fishermen.

And since I have your promise to hear me with patience, I will take a liberty to look back upon an observation that hath been made by an ingenuous and learned man, who observes that God hath been pleased to allow those whom he himselfe hath appointed, to write his holy will in holy writ, yet to express his will in such metaphors as their former affections or practise had inclined them to ; and he brings *Solomon* for an example, who before his con-version was remarkably amorous, and after by Gods ap-pointment, writ that love song† betwixt God and his church.

And if this hold in reason (as I see none to the con-trary) then it may be probably concluded, that *Moses* (whom I told you before, writ the book of *Job*) and the prophet *Amos* were both anglers, for you shal in all the

* Mat. 10.　　　† The Canticles.

old testament, find fish-hooks but twice mentioned; namely, by meek *Moses*, the friend of God; and by the humble prophet *Amos*.

Concerning which last, namely, the prophet *Amos*, I shall make but this observation, that he that shall read the humble, lowly, plain stile of that prophet, and compare it with the high, glorious, eloquent stile of the prophet *Isaiah* (though they be both equally true) may easily believe him to be a good natured, plaine fisherman.

Which I do the rather believe, by comparing the affectionate, lowly, humble epistles of S. *Peter*, S. *James*, and S. *John*, whom we know were fishers, with the glorious language and high metaphors of S. *Paul*, who we know was not.

Let me give you the example of two men more, that have lived nearer to our own times : first of Doctor *Nowel* sometimes Dean of S. *Paul's*, (in which church his monument stands yet undefaced) a man that in the reformation of Queen *Elizabeth* (not that of *Henry the VIII.*) was so noted for his meek spirit, deep learning, prudence and piety, that the then parliament and convocation, both chose, injoyned, and trusted him to be the man to make a catechism for publick use, such a one as should stand as a rule for faith and manners to their posteritie : And the good man (though he was very learned, yet knowing that God leads us not to heaven by hard questions) made that good, plain, unperplext Catechism, that is printed with the old service book. I say, this good man was as dear a lover, and constant practicer of angling, as any age can produce ; and his custome was to spend (besides his fixt hours of prayer those hours which by command of the church were enjoined the old clergy, and voluntarily dedicated to devotion by many primitive Christians :) besides those hours, this good man was observed to spend, or if you will, to bestow a tenth part of his time in angling ; and also, (for I have conversed with those which have conversed with him) to bestow a tenth part of his revenue, and all his fish, amongst the poor that inhabited near to those rivers in which it was caught, saying often *that charity gave life to religion :* and at his return would praise God he had spent that day free from worldly trouble, both harmlesly and in a recreation that became a church-man.

My next and last example shall be that undervaluer of money, the late provost of *Eaton Colledg,* Sir *Henry Wotton,* (a man with whom I have often fish'd and convers'd) a man whose forraign imployments in the service of this nation, and whose experience, learning, wit and cheerfulness, made his company to be esteemed one of the delights of mankind; this man, whose very approbation of angling were sufficient to convince any modest censurer of it, this man was also a most dear lover, and a frequent practicer of the art of angling, of which he would say "['twas an imployment for his idle time, which was not idly spent ;]" for angling was after tedious study "[a rest to his mind, a cheerer of his spirits, a divertion of sadness, a calmer of unquiet thoughts, a moderator of passions, a procurer of contentedness, and that it begot habits of peace and patience in those that profest and practic'd it]."

Sir, this was the saying of that learned man; and I do easily believe that peace, and patience, and a calm content did cohabit in the cheerful heart of Sir *Henry Wotton,* because I know, that when he was beyond seventy years of age he made this description of a part of the present pleasure that possest him, as he sate quietly in a summer's evening on a bank a fishing; it is a description of the spring, which because it glides as soft and sweetly from his pen, as that river does now by which it was then made, I shall repeat unto you.

> This day dame nature seem'd in love :
> The lustie sap began to move ;
> Fresh juice did stir th' imbracing vines,
> And birds had drawn their valentines.
> The jealous *Trout,* that low did lye,
> Rose at a well dissembled *flie ;*
> There stood my friend with patient skill,
> Attending of his trembling quil.
> Already were the eaves possest
> With the swift pilgrims dawbed nest :

The groves already did rejoice,
In *Philomels* triumphing voice :
The showrs were short, the weather mild,
The morning fresh, the evening smil'd.
 Jone takes her neat rubb'd pail, and now
She trips to milk the sand-red *cow ;*
Where, for some sturdy foot-ball swain,
Jone strokes a *sillibub* or twaine.
The field and gardens were beset
With *tulips, crocus, violet,*
And now, though late, the modest *rose*
Did more than half a blush disclose.
Thus all looks gay and full of chear
 To welcome the new liveried year.

These were the thoughts that then possest the undisturbed mind of Sir *Henry Wotton.* Will you hear the
wish of another angler,* and the commendation of his
happy life, which he also sings in verse.

Let me live harmlessly, and near the brink
Of *Trent* or *Avon* have a dwelling place,
Where I may see my *quil* or *cork* down sink,
With eager bit of *Pearch*, or *Bleak*, or *Dace* ;
And on the world and my Creator think,
Whilst some men strive, ill gotten goods t' imbrace ;
 And others spend their time in base excess
 Of wine or worse, in *war* and *wantonness.*

Let them that list these pastimes still pursue,
And on such pleasing fancies feed their fill,
So I the *fields* and *meadows* green may view,
And daily by *fresh rivers* walk at will,
Among the *daisies* and the *violets* blue,
Red *hyacinth*, and yellow *daffadil,*
 Purple *narcissus*, like the morning rayes,
 Pale *ganderglass* and azure *culverkayes.*

I count it higher pleasure to behold
The stately compass of the lofty *skie,*
And in the midst thereof (like burning gold)
The flaming chariot of the world's great eye,

    * Jo. Da.

The watery clouds, that in the aire up rold,
With sundry kinds of painted colours flye
  And fair *Aurora* lifting up her head,
  Still blushing, rise from old *Tithonius* bed.

The *hils* and *mountains* raised from the *plains,*
The *plains* extended level with the *ground,*
The *grounds* divided into sundry *vains,*
The *vains* inclos'd with *rivers* running round ;
These *rivers* making way through nature's chains
With headlong course into the sea profound ;
  The raging *sea*, beneath the vallies low,
  Where *lakes*, and *rils*, and *rivulets* do flow.

The loftie woods, the forrests wide and long
Adorn'd with leaves and branches fresh and green,
In whose cool bowres the birds with many a song
Do welcom with their quire the *Sumers Queen :*
The meadows fair, where *Flora's* gifts among
Are intermixt, with verdant grass between.
  The silver-scaled *fish* that softly swim,
  Within the sweet brooks chrystal watry stream.

All these, and many more of his creation,
That made the heavens, the *Angler* oft doth see,
Taking therein no little delectation,
To think how strange, how wonderful they be ;
Framing thereof an inward contemplation,
To set his heart from other fancies free ;
  And whilst he looks on these with joyful eye,
  His mind is rapt above the Starry Skie.

Sir, I am glad my memory did not lose these last verses, because they are somewhat more pleasant and more sutable to *May day*, then my harsh discourse, and I am glad your patience hath held out so long, as to hear them and me ; for both together have brought us within the sight of the *Thatcht House ;* and I must be your debtor (if you think it worth your attention) for the rest of my promised discourse, till some other opportunity and a like time of leisure.

Viat. Sir, you have angled me on with so much plea-

sure to the *Thatcht House,* and I now find your words
true, *that good company makes the way seem short;* for,
trust me, sir, I thought we had wanted three miles of the
Thatcht House, till you shewed it to me : but now we are
at it, we'l turn into it, and refresh our selves with a cup
of ale and a little rest.

Pisc. Most gladly (sir) and we'l drink a civil cup to
all the *Otter Hunters* that are to meet you to morrow.

Viat. That we wil, sir, and to all the lovers of angling,
too, of which number, I am now one my self, for by the
help of your good discourse and company, I have put on
new thoughts both of the art of angling, and of all that
profess it : and if you will but meet me to-morrow at the
time and place appointed, and bestow one day with me
and my friends in hunting the *Otter,* I will the next two
dayes wait upon you, and we two will for that time do
nothing but angle, and talk of fish and fishing.

Pisc. 'Tis a match, sir, I'l not fail you, God willing, to
be at *Amwel Hil* to morrow morning before sun-rising.

CHAP. II.

Viat. MY friend *Piscator,* you have kept time with my
thoughts, for the sun is just rising, and I my self just now
come to this place, and the dogs have just now put down
an *Otter,* look down at the bottom of the hil, there in that
meadow, chequered with water lillies and lady-smocks,
there you may see what work they make : look, you see
all busie, men and dogs, dogs and men, all busie.

Pisc. Sir, I am right glad to meet you, and glad to
have so fair an entrance into this dayes sport, and glad to
see so many dogs, and more men all in pursuit of the
Otter; lets complement no longer, but joine unto them ;
come honest *Viator,* lets be gone, lets make haste, I long
to be doing ; no reasonable hedge or ditch shall hold me.

Viat. Gentleman huntsman, where found you this
Otter ?

Hunt. Marry (sir) we found her a mile off this place

a fishing; she has this morning eaten the greatest part of this *Trout*, she has only left thus much of it as you see, and was fishing for more; when we came we found her just at it: but we were here very early, we were here an hour before sun-rise, and have given her no rest since we came: sure she'l hardly escape all these dogs and men. I am to have the skin if we kill him.

Viat. Why, sir, whats the skin worth?

Hunt. 'Tis worth ten shillings to make gloves; the gloves of an *Otter* are the best fortification for your hands against wet weather that can be thought of.

Pisc. I pray, honest huntsman, let me ask you a pleasant question, Do you hunt a beast or a fish?

H. Sir, It is not in my power to resolve you; for the question has been debated among many great clerks, and they seem to differ about it; but most agree that his tail is fish: and if his body be fish too, then I may say, that a fish will walk upon land (for an *Otter* does so) sometimes five or six, or ten miles in a night. But (sir) I can tell you certainly, that he devours much fish, and kils and spoils much more: and I can tell you, that he can smel a fish in the water one hundred yards from him (*Gesner* sayes, much farther) and that his stones are good against the falling-sickness: and that there is an herb *Benione*, which being hung in a linen cloth near a fish pond, or any haunt that he uses, makes him to avoid the place, which proves he can smell both by water and land. And thus much for my knowledg of the *Otter*, which you may now see above water at vent, and the dogs close with him; I now see he will not last long, follow therefore my masters, follow, for *Sweetlips* was like to have him at this vent.

Via. Oh me, all the horse are got over the river, what shall we do now?

Hun. Marry, stay a little and follow, both they and the dogs will be suddenly on this side again, I warrant you, and the *Otter* too it may be; now have at him with *Kilbuck*, for he vents again.

Via. Marry so he is, for look he vents in that corner. Now, now *Ringwood* has him. Come bring him to me. Look, 'tis a bitch *Otter* upon my word, and she has lately whelped, lets go to the place where she was *put down*, and not far from it, you will find all her young ones, I dare warrant you : and kill them all too.

Hunt. Come gentlemen, come all, lets go to the place where we *put downe* the *Otter;* look you, hereabout it was that shee kennell'd ; look you, here it was indeed, for here's her young ones, no less then five : come lets kill them all.

Pisc. No, I pray sir ; save me one, and I'll try if I can make her tame, as I know an ingenuous gentleman in *Leicester-shire* has done * ; who hath not only made her tame, but to catch fish and doe many things of much pleasure.

Hunt. Take one with all my heart ; but let us kill the rest. And now lets go to an honest alehouse and sing *Old Rose*, and rejoice all of us together.

Viat. Come my friend, let me invite you along with us ; I'll bear your charges this night, and you shall beare mine to morrow ; for my intention is to accompany you a day or two in fishing.

Pisc. Sir, your request is granted, and I shall be right glad, both to exchange such a courtesie, and also to enjoy your company.

Viat. Well, now lets go to your sport of angling.

Pisc. Lets be going with all my heart, God keep you all, gentlemen, and send you meet this day with another bitch *Otter*, and kill her merrily, and all her young ones too.

Viat. Now *Piscator*, where wil you begin to fish ?

Pisc. We are not yet come to a likely place, I must walk a mile further yet before I begin.

Viat. Well then, I pray, as we walk, tell me freely how you like my hoste, and the company ? is not mine hoste a witty man ?

Pisc. Sir, To speak truly, he is not to me ; for most of his conceits were either scripture-jests, or lascivious jests ; for which I count no man witty : for the divel will help a

* *Mr. Nich. Seagrave.*

man that way inclin'd, to the first, and his own corrupt nature (which he always carries with him) to the latter. But a companion that feasts the company with *wit* and *mirth*, and leaves out the *sin* (which is usually mixt with them) he is the man : and indeed, such a man should have his charges born : and to such company I hope to bring you this night ; for at *Trout-Hall*, not far from this place, where I purpose to lodg to night, there is usually an angler that proves good company.

But for such discourse as we heard last night, it infects others ; the very boyes will learn to talk and swear as they heard mine host, and another of the company that shall be nameless ; well, you know what example is able to do, and I know what the poet sayes in the like case :

———————Many a one
Owes to his country his religion :
And in another would as strongly grow,
Had but his nurse or mother taught him so.

This is reason put into verse, and worthy the consideration of a wise man. But of this no more, for though I love civility, yet I hate severe censures : I'll to my own art, and I doubt not but at yonder tree I shall catch a *Chub*, and then we'll turn to an honest ale house that I know right well, rest our selves, and dress it for our dinner.

Via. Oh, sir, a *Chub* is the worst fish that swims ; I hoped for a *Trout* for my dinner.

Pisc. Trust me, sir, there is not a likely place for a *Trout* hereabout, and we staid so long to take our leave of your huntsmen this morning, that the sun is got so high, and shines so clear, that I will not undertake the catching of a *Trout* till evening, and though a *Chub* be by you and many others reckoned the worst of all fish, yet you shall see I'll make it good fish by dressing it.

Viat. Why, how will you dress him ?

Pisc. I'll tell you when I have caught him : look you here, sir, do you see ? (but you must stand very close) there lye upon the top of the water twenty *Chubs :* I'll catch only one, and that shall be the biggest of them all : and that I will do so, I'll hold you twenty to one.

Viat. I marry, sir, now you talk like an artist, and I'll say, you are one, when I shall see you perform what you say you can do ; but I yet doubt it.

Pisc. And that you shall see me do presently ; look, the biggest of these *Chubs* has had some bruise upon his tail, and that looks like a white spot ; that very *Chub* I mean to catch ; sit you but down in the shade, and stay but a little while, and I'l warrant you I'l bring him to you.

Viat. I'l sit down and hope well, because you seem to be so confident.

Pisc. Look you, sir, there he is, that very *Chub* that I shewed you, with the white spot on his tail ; and I'l be as certain to make him a good dish of meat, as I was to catch him. I'l now lead you to an honest ale-house, where we shall find a cleanly room, lavender in the windowes, and twenty ballads stuck about the wall ; there my hostis (which I may tel you, is both cleanly and conveniently handsome) has drest many a one for me, and shall now dress it after my fashion, and I warrant it good meat.

Viat. Come sir, with all my heart, for I begin to be hungry, and long to be at it, and indeed to rest my self too ; for though I have walked but four miles this morning, yet I begin to be weary ; yester dayes hunting hangs stil upon me.

Pisc. Wel sir, and you shal quickly be at rest, for yonder is the house I mean to bring you to.

Come hostis, how do you ? wil you first give us a cup of your best ale, and then dress this *Chub*, as you drest my last, when I and my friend were here about eight or ten daies ago ? but you must do me one courtesie, it must be done instantly.

Host. I wil do it, Mr. *Piscator,* and with all the speed I can.

Pisc. Now sir, has not my hostis made haste ? and does not the fish look lovely ?

Viat. Both, upon my word sir, and therefore lets say grace and fall to eating of it.

Pisc. Well sir, how do you like it ?

Viat. Trust me, 'tis as good meat as ever I tasted : now

let me thank you for it, drink to you, and beg a courtesie of you ; but it must not be deny'd me.

Pisc. What is it, I pray sir? you are so modest, that me thinks I may promise to grant it before it is asked.

Viat. Why sir, it is that from henceforth you will allow me to call you master, and that really I may be your scholer, for you are such a companion, and have so quickly caught, and so excellently cook'd this fish, as makes me ambitious to be your scholer.

Pisc. Give me your hand : from this time forward I wil be your master, and teach you as much in this art as I am able ; and will, as you desire me, tel you somewhat of the nature of some of the fish which we are to angle for ; and I am sure I shal tel you more than every angler yet knows.

And first I will tel you how you shall catch such a *Chub* as this was ; and then how to cook him as this was : I could not have begun to teach you to catch any fish more easily than this fish is caught ; but then it must be this particular way, and this you must do :

Go to the same hole, where in most hot days you will finde floting neer the top of the water, at least a dozen or twenty *Chubs;* get a *Grashopper* or two as you goe, and get secretly behinde the tree, put it then upon your hook, and let your hook hang a quarter of a yard short of the top of the water, and 'tis very likely that the shadow of your rod, which you must rest on the tree, will cause the *Chubs* to sink down to the bottom with fear ; for they be a very fearful fish, and the shadow of a bird flying over them will make them do so ; but they will presently rise up to the top again, and there lie soaring till some shadow affrights them again : when they lie upon the top of the water, look out the best *Chub*, which you setting your self in a fit place, may very easily doe, and move your rod as softly as a snail moves, to that *Chub* you intend to catch ; let your bait fall gently upon the water three or four inches before him, and he will infallibly take the bait, and you will be as sure to catch him ; for hee is one of the leather-mouth'd fishes, of which a hook does scarce ever lose his hold : and therefore give him play enough before you offer

to take him out of the water.   Go your way presently, take
my rod, and doe as I bid you, and I will sit down and mend
my tackling till you return back.

Viat. Truly, my loving master, you have offered mee
as fair as I could wish : Ile goe and observe your directions.

Look you, master, what I have done ; that which joyes
my heart ; caught just such another *Chub* as yours was.

Pisc. Marry, and I am glad of it : I am like to have a
towardly scholer of you.   I now see, that with advice and
practice you wil make an *angler* in a short time.

Viat. But master, what if I could not have found a
Grashopper ?

Pisc. Then I may tel you, that a *black Snail*, with his
belly slit, to shew his white ; or a piece of soft *cheese* wil
usually do as wel ; nay, sometimes a *worm*, or any kind
of *fly ;* as the *Ant-fly*, the *Flesh-fly*, or *Wall-fly*, or the
Dor or *Beetle* (which you may find under a sod), or a *Bob*,
which you wil find in the same place, and in time wil be a
Beetle ; it is a short white worm, like to, and bigger then
a gentle ; or a *Cod-worm*, or *Case-worm :* any of these
wil do very wel to fish in such a manner.   And after this
manner you may catch a *Trout :* in a hot evening, when
as you walk by a brook, and shal see or hear him leap at
flies, then if you get a *Grashopper*, put it on your hook,
with your line about two yards long, standing behind a
bush or tree where his hole is, and make your bait stir up
and down on the top of the water ; you may, if you stand
close, be sure of a bit, but not sure to catch him, for he is
not a leather mouthed fish : and after this manner you
may fish for him with almost any kind of live flie, but
especially with a *Grashopper.*

Viat. But before you go further, I pray good master,
what mean you by a leather mouthed fish.

Pisc. By a leather mouthed fish, I mean such as have
their teeth in their throat, as the *Chub* or *Cheven*, and so
the *Barbel*, the *Gudgion* and *Carp*, and divers others have,
and the hook being stuck into the leather or skin of such
fish, does very seldome or never lose its hold : but on the
contrary, a *Pike*, a *Pearch*, or *Trout*, and so some other

fish which have not their teeth in their throats, but in their mouthes, which you shal observe to be very full of bones, and the skin very thin, and little of it : I say, of these fish the hook never takes so sure hold, but you often lose the fish unless he have gorg'd it.

Viat. I thank you good master for this observation ; but now what shal be done with my *Chub* or *Chevin* that I have caught.

Pisc. Marry sir, it shall be given away to some poor body, for Ile warrant you Ile give you a *Trout* for your supper ; and it is a good beginning o. your art to offer your first fruits to the poor, who will both thank God and you for it.

And now lets walk towards the water again, and as I go Ile tel you when you catch your next *Chub*, how to dresse it as this was.

Viat. Come (good master) I long to be going and learn your directions.

Pisc. You must dress it, or see it drest thus : When you have scaled him, wash him very cleane, cut off his tail and fins ; and wash him not after you gut him, but chine or cut him through the middle as a salt fish is cut, then give him four or five scotches with your knife, broil him upon wood-cole or char-cole ; but as he is broiling, baste him often with butter that shal be choicely good ; and put good store of salt into your butter, or salt him gently as you broil or baste him ; and bruise or cut very small into your butter, a little time, or some other sweet herb that is in the garden where you eat him : thus used, it takes away the watrish taste which the *Chub* or *Chevin* has, and makes him a choice dish of meat, as you your self know ; for thus was that dress'd, which you did eat of to your dinner.

Or you may (for variety) dress a *Chub* another way, and you will find him very good, and his tongue and head almost as good as a Carps ; but then you must be sure that no grasse or weeds be left in his mouth or throat.

Thus you must dress him : slit him through the middle, then cut him into four pieces ; then put him into a pewter dish, and cover him with another, put into him as

much white wine as wil cover him, or spring water and
vinegar, and store of salt, with some branches of time,
and other sweet herbs; let him then be boiled gently over
a chafing dish with wood coles, and when he is almost
boiled enough, put half of the liquor from him, not the
top of it; put then into him a convenient quantity of the
best butter you can get, with a little nutmeg grated into
it, and sippets of white bread : thus ordered, you wil find
the *Chevin* and the sauce too, a choice dish of meat : and
I have been the more careful to give you a perfect direction how to dress him, because he is a fish undervalued by
many, and I would gladly restore him to some of his credit
which he has lost by ill cookery.

Viat. But master, have you no other way to catch a
Chevin, or *Chub?*

Pisc. Yes that I have, but I must take time to tel it
you hereafter; or indeed, you must learn it by observation
and practice, though this way that I have taught you was
the easiest to catch a *Chub*, at this time, and at this place.
And now we are come again to the river; I wil (as the
souldier sayes) prepare for skirmish ; that is, draw out my
tackling, and try to catch a *Trout* for supper.

Viat. Trust me master, I see now it is a harder matter
to catch a *Trout* then a *Chub;* for I have put on patience,
and followed you this two hours, and not seen a fish stir,
neither at your minnow nor your worm.

Pisc. Wel scholer, you must endure worse luck sometime, or you will never make a good angler. But what
say you now? there is a *Trout* now, and a good one too,
if I can but hold him ; and two or three turns more will
tire him : now you see he lies still, and the sleight is to
land him : reach me that landing net. So (sir) now he is
mine own, what say you? is not this worth all my labour?

Viat. On my word master, this is a gallant *Trout;* what
shall we do with him ?

Pisc. Marry e'en eat him to supper : we'l go to my
hostis, from whence we came; she told me, as I was
going out of door, that my brother *Peter*, a good angler,
and a cheerful companion, had sent word he would lodg
there to night, and bring a friend with him. My hostis

has two beds, and I know you and I may have the best :
we'l rejoice with my brother *Peter* and his friends, tel tales,
or sing ballads, or make a catch, or find some harmless
sport to content us.

Viat. A match, good master, lets go to that house, for
the linnen looks white, and smels of lavender, and I long
to lye in a pair of sheets that smels so : lets be going,
good master, for I am hungry again with fishing.

Pisc. Nay, stay a little good scholer, I caught my last
Trout with a worm, now I wil put on a minow and try a
quarter of an hour about yonder trees for another, and so
walk towards our lodging. Look you scholer, thereabout
we shall have a bite presently, or not at all : have with
you (sir !) on my word I have him. Oh it is a great log-
gerheaded *Chub* : come, hang him upon that willow twig,
and let's be going. But turn out of the way a little, good
scholer, towards yonder high hedg : we'l sit whilst this
showr falls so gently upon the teeming earth, and gives a
sweeter smel to the lovely flowers that adorn the verdant
meadows.

Look, under that broad *Beech tree* I sate down when I
was last this way a fishing, and the birds in the adjoining
grove seemed to have a friendly contention with an echo,
whose dead voice seemed to live in a hollow cave, near to
the brow of that primrose hil ; there I sate, viewing the
silver streams glide silently towards their center, the tem-
pestuous sea, yet sometimes opposed by rugged roots, and
pibble stones, which broke their waves, and turned them
into fome : and sometimes viewing the harmless lambs,
some leaping securely in the cool shade, whilst others
sported themselves in the cheerful sun ; and others were
craving comfort from the swolne udders of their bleating
dams. As I thus sate, these and other sights had so fully
possest my soul, that I thought as the poet has happily
exprest it :

> I was for that time lifted above earth ;
> And possest jòyes not promis'd in my birth.

As I left this place, and entered into the next field, a
second pleasure entertained me, 'twas a handsome milk-

3

maid, that had cast away all care, and sung like a *Night-ingale;* her voice was good, and the ditty fitted for it ; 'twas that smooth song which was made by *Kit Marlow*, now at least fifty years ago ; and the milk maids mother sung an answer to it, which was made by Sir *Walter Raleigh* in his yonger dayes.

They were old fashioned poetry, but choicely good, I think much better than that now in fashion in this critical age. Look yonder, on my word, yonder they be both a milking again : I will give her the *Chub*, and perswade them to sing those two songs to us.

Pisc. God speed, good woman, I have been a fishing, and am going to *Bleak Hall* to my bed, and having caught more fish than wil sup my self and friend, wil bestow this upon you and your daughter, for I use to sel none.

Milkw. Marry God requite you sir, and we'l eat it cheerfully : wil you drink a draught of red cows milk ?

Pisc. No, I thank you : but I pray do us a courtesie that shal stand you and your daughter in nothing, and we wil think our selves stil something in your debt ; it is but to sing us a song, that was sung by you and your daughter, when I last past over this meadow, about eight or nine dayes since.

Milk. What song was it, I pray ? was it, *Come shep-herds deck your herds :* or, *As at noon* Dulcina *rested :* or *Philida flouts me ?*

Pisc. No, it is none of those : it is a song that your daughter sung the first part, and you sung the answer to it.

Milk. O I know it now, I learn'd the first part in my golden age, when I was about the age of my daughter ; and the later part, which indeed fits me best, but two or three years ago ; you shal, God willing, hear them both. Come *Maudlin*, sing the first part to the gentlemen with a merrie heart, and Ile sing the second.

The milk maids song.

Come live with me, and be my love,
And we wil all the pleasures prove
That vallies, groves, or hils, or fields,
Or woods and steepie mountains yeelds.

Where we will sit upon the *rocks*,
And see the shepherds feed our *flocks*,
By shallow *rivers*, to whose falls
Mellodious birds sing *madrigals.*

And I will make thee beds of *roses*,
And then a thousand fragrant posies,
A cap of flowers and a kirtle,
Imbroidered all with leaves of mirtle.

A gown made of the finest wool
Which from our pretty lambs we pull,
Slippers lin'd choicely for the cold,
With buckles of the purest gold.

A belt of straw and ivie buds
With coral clasps, and amber studs :
And if these pleasures may thee move,
Come live with me, and be my love.

The shepherd swains shal dance and sing
For thy delight each May morning :
If these delights thy mind may move,
Then live with me, and be my love.

Via. Trust me master, it is a choice song, and sweetly sung by honest *Maudlin :* Ile bestow Sir *Thomas Over-bury's* milk maids wish upon her, *that she may die in the spring, and have good store of flowers stuck round about her winding sheet.*

The milk maids mothers answer.

If all the world and love were young,
And truth in every shepherds tongue,
These pretty pleasures might me move,
To live with thee, and be thy love.

But time drives flocks from field to fold :
When rivers rage and rocks grow cold,
And *Philomel* becometh dumb,
The rest complains of cares to come.

The flowers do fade, and wanton fields
To wayward winter reckoning yeilds.
A honey tongue, a heart of gall,
Is fancies spring, but sorrows fall.

Thy gowns, thy shooes, thy beds of roses,
Thy cap, thy kirtle, and thy posies,
Soon break, soon wither, soon forgotten,
In folly ripe, in reason rotten.

Thy belt of straw and ivie buds,
Thy coral clasps and amber studs,
All these in me no means can move
To come to thee, and be thy love.

But could youth last, and love stil breed,
Had joyes no date, nor age no need ;
Then those delights my mind might move
To live with thee, and be thy love.

Pisc. Wel sung, good woman, I thank you, I'l give you
another dish of fish one of these dayes, and then beg
another song of you. Come scholer, let *Maudlin* alone,
do not you offer to spoil her voice. Look, yonder comes
my hostis to cal us to supper. How now? is my brother
Peter come ?

Host. Yes, and a friend with him, they are both glad to
hear you are in these parts, and long to see you, and are
hungry, and long to be at supper.

CHAP. III.

Piscat. WEL met brother *Peter*, I heard you and a
friend would lodg here to night, and that has made me
and my friend cast to lodge here too ; my friend is one
that would faine be a brother of the *Angle* : he has been
an *Angler* but this day, and I have taught him how to
catch a *Chub* by *daping* with a *grashopper*, and he has
caught a lusty one of nineteen inches' long. But I pray
you brother, who is it that is your companion ?

Peter. Brother *Piscator*, my friend is an honest country

man, and his name is *Coridon*, a most downright witty
merry companion that met me here purposely to eat a
Trout and be pleasant, and I have not yet wet my line
since I came from home : but I will fit him tomorrow
with a *Trout* for his breakfast, if the weather be any thing
like.

Pisc. Nay brother, you shall not delay him so long, for
look you here is a *Trout* will fill six reasonable bellies.
Come hostis, dress it presently, and get us what other
meat the house will afford, and give us some good ale, and
lets be merrie.

Peter. On my word, this *Trout* is in perfect season.
Come, I thank you, and here's a hearty draught to you,
and to all the brothers of the Angle, wheresoever they be,
and to my young brothers good fortune to morrow ; I will
furnish him with a rod, if you will furnish him with the
rest of the tackling, we will set him up and make him a
fisher.

And I will tel him one thing for his encouragement, that
his fortune hath made him happy to be a scholer to such
a master ; a master that knows as much both of the nature and breeding of fish, as any man ; and can also tell
him as well how to catch and cook them, from the *minow*
to the *sammon*, as any that I ever met withall.

Pisc. Trust me, brother *Peter*, I find my scholer to be
so sutable to my own humour, which is to be free and
pleasant, and civilly merry, that my resolution is to hide
nothing from him. Believe me, scholer, this is my resolution : and so here's to you a hearty draught, and to all
that love us, and the honest art of Angling.

Viat. Trust me, good master, you shall not sow your
seed in barren ground, for I hope to return you an increase
answerable to your hopes ; but however, you shal find me
obedient, and thankful, and serviceable to my best abilitie.

Pisc. 'Tis enough, honest scholer, come let's to supper.
Come my friend *Coridon*, this *Trout* looks lovely, it was
twenty-two inches when it was taken, and the belly of it
look'd some part of it as yellow as a marygold, and part of
it as white as a lily, and yet me thinks it looks better in
this good sawce.

Coridon. Indeed, honest friend, it looks well, and tastes well, I thank you for it, and so does my friend *Peter*, or else he is to blame.

Pet. Yes, and so I do, we all thank you, and when we have supt, I will get my friend *Coridon* to sing you a song for requital.

Cor. I wil sing a song if any body wil sing another; else, to be plain with you, I wil sing none : I am none of those that sing for meat, but for company; I say, 'tis merry in hall, when men sing all.

Pisc. I'l promise you I'l sing a song that was lately made at my request by Mr. *William Basse*, one that has made the choice songs of the *Hunter in his carrere*, and *Tom of Bedlam*, and many others of note ; and this that I wil sing is in praise of angling.

Cor. And then mine shall be the praise of a country man's life. What will the rest sing of?

Pet. I wil promise you I wil sing another song in praise of angling, to-morrow night, for we wil not part till then, but fish to-morrow, and sup together, and the next day every man leave fishing, and fall to his business.

Viat. 'Tis a match, and I wil provide you a song or a ketch against then too, that shal give some addition of mirth to the company ; for we wil be merrie.

Pisc. 'Tis a match, my masters ; let's ev'n say grace, and turn to the fire, drink the other cup to wet our whistles, and so sing away all sad thoughts.

Come on my masters, who begins? I think it is best to draw cuts and avoid contention.

Pet. It is a match. Look, the shortest cut falls to *Coridon.*

Cor. Well then, I will begin ; for I hate contention.

CORIDON'S song.

Oh the sweet contentment
The country man doth find
high trolollie loliloe
high trolollie lee,
That quiet contemplation
Possesseth all my mind :

Then care away,
and wend along with me.

For courts are full of flattery,
As hath too oft been tri'd ;
   high trolollie lollie loe
   high trolollie lee,
The city full of wantonness,
And both are full of pride.
   Then care away,
   and wend along with me..

But oh the honest country man
Speaks truly from his heart,
   high trolollie lollie loe
   high trolollie lee,
His pride is in his tillage,
His horses and his cart :
   Then care away,
   and wend along with me.

Our clothing is good sheep skins
Gray russet for our wives,
   high trolollie lollie loe
   high trolollie lee.
'Tis warmth and not gay clothing
That doth prolong our lives ;
   Then care away,
   and wend along with me.

The ploughman, though he labor hard
Yet on the *holy-day,*
   high trolollie lollie loe
   high trolollie lee,
No *emperor* so merrily
Does pass his time away ;
   Then care away,
   and wend along with me.

To recompense our tillage,
The *heavens* afford us show'rs ;
   high trolollie lollie loe
   high trolollie lee,

And for our sweet refreshments
The earth affords us bowers :
 Then care away,
 and wend along with me.

The *cuckoe* and the *nightingale*
Full merrily do sing,
 high trolollie lollie loe
 high trolollie lee,
And with their pleasant *roundelayes,*
Bid welcome to the *spring :*
 Then care away,
 and wend along with me.

This is not half the happiness
The country man injoyes ;
 high trolollie lollie loe
 high trolollie lee,
Though others think they have as much
Yet he that sayes so lies :
 Then come away, turn
 Country man with me.

Pisc. Well sung *Coridon*, this song was sung with mettle, and it was choicely fitted to the occasion ; I shall love you for it as long as I know you. I would you were a brother of the angle ; for a companion that is cheerful and free from swearing and scurrilous discourse, is worth gold. I love such mirth as does not make friends ashamed to look upon one another next morning ; nor men (that cannot wel bear it) to repent the money they spend when they be warmed with drink : and take this for a rule, you may pick out such times and such companies, that you may make your selves merrier for a little than a great deal of money ; for *'tis the company and not the charge that makes the feast:* and such a companion you prove, I thank you for it.

But I will not compliment you out of the debt that I owe you, and therefore I will begin my song, and wish it may be as well liked.

The ANGLER'S song.

As inward love breeds outward talk,
The *hound* some praise, and some the *hawk*,
Some better pleas'd with private sport,
Use *Tenis*, some a *Mistris* court :
  But these delights I neither wish,
  Nor envy, while I freely fish.

Who *hunts*, doth oft in danger ride ;
Who *hauks*, lures oft both far and wide ;
Who uses *games*, may often prove
A loser ; but who fals in love,
  Is fettered in fond *Cupid's* snare :
  My angle breeds me no such care.

Of recreation there is none
So free as fishing is alone ;
All other pastimes do no less
Than mind and body both possess ;
  My hand alone my work can do,
  So I can fish and study too.

I care not, I, to fish in seas,
Fresh rivers best my mind do please,
Whose sweet calm course I contemplate,
And seek in life to imitate ;
  In civil bounds I fain would keep,
  And for my past offences weep.

And when the timerous *Trout* I wait
To take, and he devours my bait,
How poor a thing sometimes I find
Will captivate a greedy mind :
  And when none bite, I praise the wise,
  Whom vain allurements ne're surprise.

But yet though while I fish, I fast,
I make good fortune my repast,
And thereunto my friend invite,
In whom I more than that delight :
  Who is more welcome to my dish,
  Than to my angle was my fish.

As well content no prize to take
As use of taken prize to make;
For so our Lord was pleased when
He fishers made fishers of men;
   Where (which is in no other game)
   A man may fish and praise his name.

The first men that our Saviour dear
Did chuse to wait upon him here,
Blest fishers were; and fish the last
Food was that he on earth did taste:
   I therefore strive to follow those,
   Whom he to follow him hath chose.

W. B.

Cor. Well sung brother, you have paid your debt in good coyn, we anglers are all beholding to the good man that made this song. Come hostis, give us more ale and lets drink to him.

And now lets everie one go to bed that we may rise early; but first lets pay our reckoning, for I will have nothing to hinder me in the morning, for I will prevent the sun-rising.

Pet. A match: come *Coridon*, you are to be my bed-fellow: I know brother you and your scholer wil lie together; but where shal we meet to-morrow night? for my friend *Coridon* and I will go up the water towards *Ware*.

Pisc. And my scholer and I will go down towards *Waltham*.

Cor. Then lets meet here, for here are fresh sheets that smel of lavender, and, I am sure, we cannot expect better meat and better usage.

Pet. 'Tis a match. Good night to every body.

Pisc. And so say I.

Viat. And so say I.

Pisc. Good morrow good hostis, I see my brother *Peter* is in bed still; come, give my scholer and me a cup of ale, and be sure you get us a good dish of meat against supper, for we shall come hither as hungry as *hawks*. Come scholer, lets be going.

Viat. Good master, as we walk towards the water, wil you be pleased to make the way seeme shorter by telling me first the nature of the *Trout*, and then how to catch him.

Pisc. My honest scholer, I will do it freely : the *Trout* (for which I love to angle above any fish) may be justly said (as the ancient poets say of wine, and we English say of venson) to be a generous fish, because he has his seasons, a fish that comes in, and goes out with the *stag* or *buck;* and you are to observe, that as there be some *barren does*, that are good in summer ; so there be some *barren Trouts*, that are good in winter ; but there are not many that are so, for usually they be in their perfection in the month of *May*, and decline with the *buck:* now you are to take notice, that in several countries, as in *Germany* and in other parts compar'd to ours, they differ much in their bigness, shape, and other wayes, and so do *Trouts;* 'tis wel known that in the Lake *Lemon*, the Lake of *Geneva*, there are *Trouts* taken, of three cubits long, as is affirmed by *Gesner*, a writer of good credit : and *Mercator* sayes, the *Trouts* that are taken in the Lake of *Geneva*, are a great part of the merchandize of that famous city. And you are further to know, that there be certaine waters that breed *Trouts* remarkable, both for their number and smalness. I know a little brook in *Kent* that breeds them to a number incredible, and you may take them twentie or fortie in an hour, but none greater than about the size of a *Gudgion.* There are also in divers rivers, especially that relate to, or be near to the sea, (as *Winchester*, or the Thames about *Windsor*) a little *Trout* called a *Samlet* or *Skegger Trout* (in both which places I have caught twentie or fortie at a standing) that will bite as fast and as freely as *Minnows;* these be by some taken to be young *Salmons*, but in those waters they never grow to bee bigger than a *Herring.*

There is also in *Kent*, neer to *Canterbury*, a *Trout* (called there a *Fordig Trout*) a *Trout* (that bears the name of the town where 'tis usually caught) that is accounted rare meat, many of them near the bigness of a *Salmon*, but knowne by their different colour, and in their best season cut very white; and none have been known to be caught with an angle, unless it were one that was caught by honest Sir *George Hastings*, an excellent angler (and now with God) and he has told me, he thought that *trout* bit not for hunger, but wantonness; and 'tis the rather to be believed, because both he then, and many others before him have been curious to search into their bellies what the food was by which they lived; and have found out nothing by which they might satisfie their curiositie.

Concerning which you are to take notice, that it is reported, there is a fish that hath not any mouth, but lives by taking breath by the porins of her gils, and feeds and is nourish'd by no man knows what; and this may be believed of the *Fordig Trout*, which as it is said of the *stork*, that he knowes his season, so he knows his times (I think almost his day) of coming into the river out of the sea, where he lives (and it is like feeds) nine months of the year, and about three in the river of *Fordig*.

And now for some confirmation of this; you are to know, that this *Trout* is thought to eat nothing in the fresh water; and it may be the better believed, because it is well known, that *swallowes*, which are not seen to flye in *England* for six months in the year, but about *Michaelmas* leave us for a hotter climate; yet some of them, that have been left behind their fellows[*], have been found (many thousand at a time) in hollow trees, where they have been observed to live and sleep out the whole winter without meat; and so *Albertus* observes that there is one kind of *frog*[†] that hath her mouth naturally shut up about the end of *August*, and that she lives so all the winter, and though it be strange to some, yet it is known to too many amongst us to bee doubted.

And so much for these *Fordig Trouts*, which never afford an *Angler* sport, but either live their time of being in the fresh water by their meat formerly gotten in the sea, (not unlike the *swallow* or *frog*) or by the vertue of the fresh water only, as the *Camelion* is said to live by the air.

There is also in *Northumberland*, a *Trout*, called a

---

[*] View Sir *Fra. Bacon* exper. 899.   [†] See *Topsel* of *Frogs*.

Bull Trout, of a much greater length and bignesse than any in these southern parts ; and there is in many rivers that relate to the sea, *Salmon Trouts* as much different one from another, both in shape and in their spots, as we see sheep differ one from another in their shape and bigness, and in the finess of their wool : and certainly as some pastures do breed larger sheep, so do some rivers, by reason of the ground over which they run, breed larger *Trouts.*

Now the next thing that I will commend to your consideration is, that the *Trout* is of a more sudden growth than other fish : concerning which you are also to take notice, that he lives not so long as the *Pearch* and divers other fishes do, as Sir *Francis Bacon* hath observed in his history of life and death.

And next, you are to take notice, that after hee is come to his full growth, he declines in his bodie, but keeps his bigness or thrives in his head till his death. And you are to know that he wil about (especially before) the time of his spawning, get almost miraculously through *weires* and *floud-gates* against the stream, even through such high and swift places as is almost incredible. Next, that the *Trout* usually spawns about *October* or *November*, but in some rivers a little sooner or later ; which is the more observable, because most other fish spawne in the spring or summer, when the sun hath warmed both the earth and water, and made it fit for generation.

And next, you are to note, that till the sun gets to such a height as to warm the earth and the water, the *Trout* is sick, and lean, and lowsie, and unwholesome : for you shall in winter find him to have a big head, and then to be lank, and thin, and lean ; at which time many of them have sticking on them sugs, or *Trout* lice, which is a kind of a worm, in shape like a clove or a pin, with a big head, and sticks close to him and sucks his moisture ; those I think the *Trout* breeds himselfe, and never thrives til he free himself from them, which is not till warm weather comes, and then as he growes stronger, he gets from the dead, still water, into the sharp streames and the gravel, and there rubs off these worms or lice : and then as he grows stronger, so he gets him into swifter and swifter streams, and there lies at the watch for any flie or minow that comes neer to him ; and he especially loves the *May* flie, which is bred of the *Cod-worm* or *Caddis ;* and these make the *Trout* bold and lustie, and he is usually fatter, and better meat at the end of that month, than at any time of the year.

Now you are to know, that it is observed, that usually the best *Trouts* are either red or yellow, though some be white and yet good ; but that is not usual ; and it is a note observable that the female *Trout* hath usually a less head and a deeper body than the male *Trout ;* and a little head to any fish, either *Trout, Salmon,* or other fish, is a sign that that fish is in season.

But yet you are to note, that as you see some willows or palm trees bud and blossome sooner than others do, so some *Trouts* be in some rivers sooner in season ; and as the holly or oak are longer before they cast their leaves, so are some *Trouts* in some rivers longer before they go out of season.

CHAP. IV.

AND having told you these observations concerning *Trouts,* I shall next tell you how to catch them : which is usually with a *worm,* or a *minnow* (which some call a *Penke ;*) or with a *flie,* either a *natural* or an *artificial* flie : concerning which three I wil give you some observations and directions.

For worms, there be very many sorts ; some bred onely in the earth, as the *earth worm ;* others amongst or of plants, as the *dug worm ;* and others in the bodies of living creatures ; or some of dead fish, as the *magot* or *gentle,* and others.

Now these be most of them particularly good for particular fishes : but for the *Trout* the *dew-worm,* (which some also cal the *lob-worm*) and the *brandling* are the chief; and especially the first for a great Trout, and the later for a lesse. There be also of *lob-worms*, some called *squirel-tails* (a worm which has had a red head, a streak down the back, and a broad tail) which are noted to be the best, because they are the toughest, and most lively, and live longest in the water : for you are to know, that a dead worm is but a dead bait, and like to catch nothing, compared to a lively, quick, stirring worm : and for a *brandling*, hee is usually found in an old dung-hil, or some very rotten place neer to it ; but most usually in cow dung, or hogs dung, rather than horse dung, which is somewhat too hot and dry for that worm.

There are also divers other kindes of worms, which for colour and shape alter even as the ground out of which they are got : as the *marsh-worm*, the *tag-tail*, the *flag-worm*, the *dock-worm*, the *oake-worm*, the *gilt-tail*, and too many to name, even as many sorts, as some think there be of severall kinds of birds in the air : of which I shall say no more, but tell you, that what worms soever you fish with, are the better for being long kept before they be used ; and in case you have not been so provident, then the way to cleanse and scoure them quickly, is to put them all night in water, if they be lob-worms, and then put them into your bag with fennel : but you must not put your brandling above an hour in water, and then put them into fennel for sudden use : but if you have time, and purpose to keep them long, then they be best preserved in an earthen pot with good store of *mosse*, which is to be fresh every week or eight dayes ; or at least taken from them, and clean wash'd, and wrung betwixt your hands till it be dry, and then put it to them again : and for moss, you are to note, that there be divers kindes of it, which I could name to you, but wil onely tel you, that that which is likest a *Bucks horn* is the best; except it be *white* moss, which grows on some heaths, and is hard to be found.

For the *minnow* or *penke*, he is easily found and caught in April, for then hee appears in the rivers : but nature hath taught him to shelter and hide himself in the winter in ditches that be neer to the river, and there both to hide and keep himself warm in the weeds, which rot not so so soon as in a running river; in which place if hee were in winter, the distempered floods that are usually in that season, would suffer him to have no rest, but carry him headlong to mils and weires to his confusion. And of these *minnows*, first you are to know, that the biggest size is not the best; and next, that the middle size and the whitest are the best: and then you are to know, that I cannot well teach in words, but must shew you how to put it on your hook, that it may turn the better: and you are also to know, that it is impossible it should turn too quick: and you are yet to know, that in case you want a minnow, then a small *loch*, or a *sticklebag*, or any other small fish will serve as wel: and you are yet to know, that you may salt, and by that means keep them fit for use three or four dayes or longer: and that of salt, bay salt is the best.

Now for *flies*, which is the third bait wherewith *Trouts* are usually taken. You are to know, that there are as many sorts of flies as there be of fruits: I will name you but some of them: as the *dun flie*, the *stone flie*, the *red flie*, the *moor flie*, the *tawny flie*, the *shel flie*, the *cloudy* or blackish *flie:* there be of flies, *caterpillars*, and *canker flies*, and *bear flies;* and indeed, too many either for mee to name, or for you to remember: and their breeding is so various and wonderful, that I might easily amaze my self, and tire you in a relation of them.

And yet I wil exercise your promised patience by saying a little of the *caterpillar*, or the *palmer flie* or *worm;* that by them you may guess what a work it were in a discourse but to run over those very many *flies*, *worms*, and little living creatures with which the sun and summer adorn and beautifie the river banks and meadows; both for the recreation and contemplation of the angler: and which (I think) I my self enjoy more than any other man that is not of my profession.

Pliny holds an opinion, that many have their birth or being from a dew that in the spring falls upon the leaves of trees; and that some kinds of them are from a dew left upon herbs or flowers, and others from a dew left upon colworts or cabbages: all which kindes of dews

being thickened and condensed, are by the suns generative heat most of them hatch'd, and in three dayes made
living creatures, and of several shapes and colours ; some
being hard and tough, some smooth and soft ; some are
horned in their head, some in their tail, some have none :
some have hair, some none ; some have sixteen feet, some
less, and some have none ; but (as our *Topsel** hath with
great diligence observed) those which have none, move
upon the earth, or upon broad leaves, their motion being
not unlike to the waves of the sea. Some of them hee
also observes to be bred of the eggs of other caterpillers :
and that those in their time turn to be *butter-flies ;* and
again, that their eggs turn the following yeer to be *caterpillers.*

'Tis endlesse to tell you what the curious searchers into
natures productions, have observed of these worms and
flies : but yet I shall tell you what our *Topsel* sayes of the
canker, or *palmer-worm,* or *caterpiller ;* that whereas
others content themselves to feed on particular herbs or
leaves (for most think, those very leaves that gave them
life and shape, give them a particular feeding and nourish-
ment, and that upon them they usually abide ;) yet he observes, that this is called a *pilgrim* or *palmer-worm,* for
his very wandering life and various food ; not contenting
himself (as others do) with any certain place for his abode,
nor any certain kinde of herb or flower for his feeding ;
but will boldly and disorderly wander up and down, and
not endure to be kept to a diet, or fixt to a particular place.

Nay, the very colours of *caterpillers* are, as one has
observed, very elegant and beautiful : I shal (for the taste
of the rest) describe one of them, which I will sometime
the next month, shew you feeding on a willow tree, and
you shall find him punctually to answer this very description : "His lips and mouth somewhat yellow, his eyes
black as jet, his fore-head purple, his feet and hinder
parts green, his tail two forked and black, the whole body
stain'd with a kind of red spots which run along the neck
and shoulder-blades, not unlike the form of a cross, or
the letter X, made thus cross-wise, and a white line drawn

* In his History of Serpents.

4

down his back to his tail ; all which add much beauty to his whole body." And it is to me observable, that at a fix'd age this *caterpiller* gives over to eat, and towards winter comes to be covered over with a strange shell or crust, and so lives a kind of dead life, without eating all the winter,* and (as others of several kinds turn to be several kinds of flies and vermin, the spring following) so this *caterpiller* then turns to be a painted butterflye.

Come, come my Scholer, you see the river stops our morning walk, and I wil also here stop my discourse, only as we sit down under this honey-suckle hedge, whilst I look a line to fit the rod that our brother *Peter* has lent you, I shall for a little confirmation of what I have said, repeat the observation of the Lord *Bartas.*

God not contented to each kind to give,
And to infuse the vertue generative,
By his wise power made many creatures breed
Of liveless bodies, without *Venus* deed.

So the cold humour breeds the *Salamander*
Who (in effect) like to her births commander,
With child with hundred winters, with her touch
Quencheth the fire, though glowing ne'r so much.

So in the fire in burning furnace springs
The fly *Perausta* with the flaming wings ;
Without the fire it dies, in it, it joyes,
Living in that which all things else destroyes.

So slow *Boötes* underneath him sees
In th'icie islands *Goslings* hatcht of trees,†
Whose fruitful leaves falling into the water,
Are turn'd ('tis known) to living fowls soon after.

So rotten planks of broken ships, do change
To *Barnacles.*   Oh transformation strange !
'Twas first a green tree, then a broken hull,
Lately a mushroom, now a flying gull.

Viat. Oh my good master, this morning walk has been spent to my great pleasure and wonder : but I pray, when

* View Sir *Fra. Bacon* Exper. 728 and 90. in his Natural History.
† Gerh. Herbal. Cambden.

shall I have your direction how to make artificial flyes, like to those that the *Trout* loves best ? and also how to use them ?

Pisc. My honest scholer, it is now past five of the clock, we will fish til nine, and then go to breakfast : go you to yonder *Sycamore tree,* and hide your bottle of drink under the hollow root of it ; for about that time, and in that place, we wil make a brave breakfast with a piece or powdered beef, and a radish or two that I have in my fish-bag ; we shall, I warrant you, make a good honest, whol-some, hungry breakfast, and I will give you direction for the making and using of your fly : and in the mean time, there is your rod and line ; and my advice is, that you fish as you see mee do, and lets try which can catch the first fish.

Viat. I thank you, master, I will observe and practice your direction as far as I am able.

Pisc. Look you scholer, you see I have hold of a good fish : I now see it is a *Trout ;* I pray put that net under him, and touch not my line, for if you do, then wee break all. Well done, scholer, I thank you. Now for an other. Trust me, I have another bite : come scholer, come lay down your rod, and help me to land this as you did the other. So, now we shall be sure to have a good dish of fish for supper.

Viat. I am glad of that, but I have no fortune ; sure master yours is a better rod, and better tackling.

Pisc. Nay then, take mine, and I will fish with yours. Look you, scholer, I have another : come, do as you did before. And now I have a bite at another. Oh me he has broke all, there's half a line and a good hook lost.

Viat. Master, I can neither catch with the first nor second angle ; I have no fortune.

Pisc. Look you, scholer, I have yet another : and now having caught three brace of *Trouts,* I will tel you a short tale as we walk towards our breakfast. A scholer (a preacher I should say) that was to preach to procure the approbation of a parish, that he might be their lecturer, had got from a fellow pupil of his the copy of a sermon that was first preached with a great commendation by him

4—2

that composed and preach it; and though the borrower of it preacht it word for word, as it was at first, yet it was utterly dislik'd as it was preach'd by the second; which the sermon borrower complained of to the lender of it, and was thus answered: I lent you indeed my *fiddle*, but not my *fiddlestick*; and you are to know, that every one cannot make musick with my words which are fitted for my own mouth. And so my scholer, you are to know, that as the ill pronunciation or ill accenting of a word in a sermon spoiles it, so the ill carriage of your line, or not fishing even to a foot in a right place, makes you lose your labour: and you are to know, that though you have my fiddle, that is, my very rod and tacklings with which you see I catch fish, yet you have not my fiddlestick, that is, skill to know how to carry your hand and line; and this must be taught you (for you are to remember I told you angling is an art) either by practice, or a long observation, or both.

But now lets say grace, and fall to breakfast; what say you scholer, to the providence of an old angler? Does not this meat taste well; and was not this place well chosen to eat it? for this *Sycamore* tree will shade us from the suns heat.

Viat. All excellent, good master, and my stomack excellent too; I have been at many costly dinners that have not afforded me half this content: and now good master, to your promised direction for making and ordering my artificiall flye.

Pisc. My honest scholer, I will do it, for it is a debt due unto you, by my promise: and because you shall not think your self more engaged to me than indeed you really are, therefore I will tell you freely, I find Mr. *Thomas Barker* (a gentleman that has spent much time and money in angling) deal so judicially and freely in a little book of his of angling, and especially of making and angling with a *flye* for a *Trout*, that I will give you his very directions without much variation, which shal follow.

Let your rod be light, and very gentle, I think the best are of two pieces; the line should not exceed (especially

for three or four links towards the hook), I say, not exceed three or four haires ; but if you can attain to angle
with one haire, you will have more rises, and catch more
fish. Now you must bee sure not to cumber yourself with
too long a line, as most do : and before you begin to
angle, cast to have the wind on your back, and the sun
(if it shines) to be before you (and to fish down the
streame), and carry the point or top of the rod downe-
ward ; by which meanes the shadow of your selfe, and
rod too will be the least offensive to the fish, for the sight
of any shadow amazes the fish, and spoiles your sport, of
which you must take a great care.

In the middle of *March* (till which time a man should
not in honestie catch a *Trout*) or in *April*, if the weather
be dark, or a little windy, or cloudie, the best fishing is
with the *palmer-worm*, of which I last spoke to you ; but
of these there be divers kinds, or at least of divers colours,
these and the *May-fly* are the ground of all *fly*-angling,
which are to be thus made :

First you must arm your hook, with the line in the in-
side of it ; then take your scissors and cut so much of
a browne *malards* feather as in your own reason wil make
the wings of it, you having withall regard to the bigness
or littleness of your hook, then lay the outmost part of
your feather next to your hook, then the point of your
feather next the shank of your hook ; and having so done,
whip it three or four times about the hook with the same
silk, with which your hook was armed, and having made
the silk fast, take the hackel of a *cock* or *capons* neck, or
a *plovers* top, which is usually better ; take off the one
side of the feather, and then take the hackel, silk or crewel,
gold or silver thred, make these fast at the bent of the
hook, (that is to say, below your arming) then you must
take the hackel, the silver or gold thred, and work it up
to the wings, shifting or stil removing your fingers as you
turn the silk about the hook : and still looking at every
stop or turne that your gold, or what materials soever you
make your *fly* of, do lye right and neatly ; and if you find
they do so, then when you have made the head, make all
fast, and then work your hackel up to the head, and make

that fast; and then with a needle or pin divide the wing
into two, and then with the arming silk whip it about
crosswayes betwixt the wings, and then with your thumb
you must turn the point of the feather towards the bent
of the hook, and then work three or four times about the
shank of the hook, and then view the proportion, and if
all be neat, and to your liking, fasten.

I confess, no direction can be given to make a man of
a dull capacity able to make a flye well; and yet I know
this, with a little practice, wil help an ingenuous angler in
a good degree; but to see a fly made by another, is the
best teaching to make it, and then an ingenuous angler
may walk by the river and mark what fly falls on the
water that day, and catch one of them, if he see *Trouts*
leap at a fly of that kind, and having alwaies hooks ready
hung with him, and having a bag also, alwaies with him
with bears hairs, or the hair of a brown or sad coloured
heifer, hackels of a cock or capon, several coloured silk
and crewel to make the body of the fly, the feathers of a
drakes head, black or brown sheeps wool, or hogs wool,
or hair, thred of gold, and of silver; silk of several colours (especially sad coloured to make the head :) and
there be also other colour'd feathers both of birds and of
peckled fowl. I say, having those with him in a bag, and
trying to make a flye, though he miss at first, yet shal he
at last hit it better, even to a perfection which none can
well teach him; and if he hit to make his *flie* right, and
have the luck to hit also where there is store of *Trouts*,
and a right wind, he shall catch such store of them, as
will encourage him to grow more and more in love with
the art of *flie-making*.

Viat. But my loving master, if any wind will not serve,
then I wish I were in *Lapland*, to buy a good wind of one
of the honest witches, that sell so many winds, and so
cheap.

Pisc. Marry scholer, but I would not be there, nor indeed from under this tree; for look how it begins to rain,
and by the clouds (if I mistake not) we shall presently
have a smoaking showre; and therefore sit close, this
Sycamore tree will shelter us; and 1 will tell you, as they

shall come into my mind, more observations of flie-fishing
for a *Trout.*

But first, for the winde ; you are to take notice that of
the windes the *south winde* is said to be the best. One
observes, that

> When the winde is south,
> It blows your bait into a fishes mouth.

Next to that, the *west* winde is believed to be the best :
and having told you that the *east* winde is the worst, I
need not tell you which winde is best in the third degree :
And yet (as *Solomon* observes, that) *hee that considers the
winde shall never sow :* so hee that busies his head too
much about them, (if the weather be not made extreme
cold by an east winde) shall be a little superstitious : for
as it is observed by some, that there is no good horse of
a bad colour ; so I have observed, that if it be a cloudy
day, and not extreme cold, let the winde sit in what corner
it will, and do its worst. And yet take this for a rule,
that I would willingly fish on the lee-shore : and you are
to take notice, that the fish lies, or swimms neerer the
bottom in winter than in summer, and also neerer the
bottom in any cold day.

But I promised to tell you more of the flie-fishing for a
Trout, (which I may have time enough to do, for you see
it rains *May-butter*). First for a *May-flie,* you may make
his body with greenish coloured crewel, or willow colour ;
darkning it in most places, with waxed silk, or rib'd with
a black haire, or some of them rib'd with silver thred ;
and such wings for the colour as you see the flie to have
at that season ; nay at that very day on the water. Or
you may make the *Oak-flie* with an orange-tawny and
black ground, and the brown of a mallards feather for the
wings ; and you are to know, that these two are most
excellent *flies,* that is, the *May-flie* and the *Oak-flie :* And
let me again tell you, that you keep as far from the water
as you can possibly, whether you fish with a flie or worm,
and fish down the streame ; and when you fish with a flie,
if it be possible, let no part of your line touch the water,
but your flie only ; and be stil moving your fly upon the

water, or casting it into the water ; you your self, being also alwaies moving down the stream. Mr. *Barker* commends severall sorts of the palmer flies, not only those rib'd with silver and gold, but others that have their bodies all made of black, or some with red, and a red hackel ; you may also make the *hawthorn-flie*, which is all black and not big, but very smal, the smaller the better ; or the *Oak-fly*, the body of which is orange colour and black crewel, with a brown wing, or a *fly* made with a peacocks feather, is excellent in a bright day : you must be sure you want not in your *magazin* bag, the peacocks feather, and grounds of such wool, and crewel as will make the grashopper : and note, that usually, the smallest flies are best ; and note also, that the light flie does usually make most sport in a dark day : and the darkest and least flie in a bright or cleare day ; and lastly note, that you are to repaire upon any occasion to your *magazin bag*, and upon any occasion vary and make them according to your fancy.

And now I shall tell you, that the fishing with a naturall flie is excellent, and affords much pleasure ; they may be found thus, the *May-fly* usually in and about that month neer to the river side, especially against rain ; the *Oak-fly* on the butt or body of an *Oak* or *Ash*, from the beginning of *May* to the end of *August* it is a brownish fly, and easie to be so found, and stands usually with his head downward, that is to say, towards the root of the tree ; the smal black fly, or *hawthorn* fly is to be had on any hawthorn bush, after the leaves be come forth ; with these and a short line (as I shewed to angle for a *Chub*) you may dap or dop, and also with a *Grashopper*, behind a tree, or in any deep hole, still making it to move on the top of the water, as if it were alive, and still keeping your self out of sight, you shall certainly have sport if there be *Trouts;* yea in a hot day, but especially in the evening of a hot day.

And now, scholer, my direction for fly-fishing is ended with this showre, for it has done raining, and now look about you, and see how pleasantly that meadow looks, nay and the earth smels as sweetly too. Come let me tell you what holy Mr. *Herbert* saies of such dayes and flowers as these, and then we will thank God that we enjoy them, and walk to the river and sit down quietly and try to catch the other brace of *Trouts.*

Sweet day, so cool, so calm, so bright,
The bridal of the earth and skie,
Sweet dews shal weep thy fall to night,
for thou must die.

Sweet rose, whose hew angry and brave
Bids the rash gazer wipe his eye,
Thy root is ever in its grave,
and thou must die.

Sweet spring, ful of sweet days and roses
A box where sweets compacted lie ;
My musick shewes you have your closes
and all must die.

Only a sweet and vertuous soul,
Like seasoned timber never gives,
But when the whole world turns to cole,
then chiefly lives.

Viat. I thank you, good master, for your good direction for fly-fishing, and for the sweet enjoyment of the pleasant day, which is so far spent without offence to God or man : and I thank you for the sweet close of your discourse with Mr. *Herberts* verses, which I have heard, loved angling ; and I do the rather believe it, because he had a spirit suitable to anglers, and to those primitive Christians that you love, and have so much commended.

Pisc. Well, my loving scholer, and I am pleased to know that you are so well pleased with my direction and discourse ; and I hope you will be pleased too, if you find a *Trout* at one of our angles which we left in the water to fish for it self ; you shall chuse which shall be yours, and it is an even lay, one catches : and let me tell you, this kind of fishing, and laying night-hooks, are like putting money to use, for they both work for the owners, when they do nothing but sleep, or eat, or rejoice, as you know

we have done this last hour, and sate as quietly and as
free from cares under this *Sycamore,* as *Virgils Tityrus*
and his *Melibæus* did under their broad *Beech* tree : no
life, my honest scholer, no life so happy and so pleasant
as the anglers, unless it be the beggers life in Summer ;
for then only they take no care, but are as happy as we
anglers.

Viat. Indeed master, and so they be, as is witnessed by
the beggers song, made long since by *Frank Davison,* a
good poet, who was not a begger, though he were a good
poet.

Pisc. Can you sing it, scholer?

Viat. Sit down a little, good master, and I wil try.

> Bright shines the sun, play, beggers, play,
> Here's scraps enough to serve to day :
> What noise of viols is so sweet
> As when our merry clappers ring?
> What mirth doth want when beggers meet?
> A beggers life is for a king :
> Eat, drink and play, sleep when we list,
> Go where we will so stocks be mist.
> Bright shines the sun, play beggers, &c.

> The world is ours and ours alone,
> For we alone have world at will ;
> We purchase not, all is our own,
> Both fields and streets we beggers fill :
> Play beggers play, play beggers play,
> Here's scraps enough to serve to day.

> A hundred herds of black and white
> Upon our gowns securely feed,
> And yet if any dare us bite,
> He dies therefore as sure as creed :
> Thus beggers lord it as they please,
> And only beggers live at ease :
> Bright shines the sun, play beggers play,
> Here's scraps enough to serve to day.

Pisc. I thank you good scholer, this song was well hu-
mor'd by the maker, and well remembred and sung by

you; and I pray forget not the ketch which you promised to make against night, for our country man honest *Coridon* will expect your ketch and my song, which I must be forc'd to patch up, for it is so long since I learnt it, that I have forgot a part of it. But come, let's stretch our legs a little in a gentle walk to the river, and try what interest our angles wil pay us for lending them so long to be used by the *Trouts*.

Viat. Oh me, look you master, a fish, a fish.

Pisc. I marry sir, that was a good fish indeed; if I had had the luck to have taken up that rod, 'tis twenty to one he should not have broke my line by running to the rods end, as you suffered him; I would have held him, unless he had been fellow to the great *Trout* that is neer an ell long, which had his picture drawne, and now to be seen at mine hoste *Rickabies* at the *George* in *Ware;* and it may be, by giving that *Trout* the Rod, that is, by casting it to him into the water, I might have caught him at the long run, for so I use alwaies to do when I meet with an overgrown fish, and you will learn to do so hereafter; for I tell you, scholer, fishing is an art, or at least, it is an art to catch fish.

Viat. But, master, will this *Trout* die, for it is like he has the hook in his belly?

Pisc. I wil tel you, scholer, that unless the hook be fast in his very gorge, he wil live, and a little time with the help of the water, wil rust the hook, and it wil in time wear away as the gravel does in the horse hoof, which only leaves a false quarter.

And now scholer, lets go to my rod. Look you scholer, I have a fish too, but it proves a logger-headed *Chub;* and this is not much a miss, for this will pleasure some poor body, as we go to our lodging to meet our brother *Peter* and *Coridon.* Come, now bait your hook again, and lay it into the water, for it rains again, and we wil ev'n retire to the *Sycamore* tree, and there I wil give you more directions concerning fishing; for I would fain make you an artist.

Viat. Yes, good-master, I pray let it be so.

CHAP. V.

Pisc. WEL, scholer, now we are sate downe and are at ease, I shall tel you a little more of *Trout* fishing before I speak of the *Salmon*, (which I purpose shall be next) and then of the *Pike* or *Luce.* You are to know, there is night as well as day-fishing for a *Trout*, and that then the best are out of their holds ; and the manner of taking them is on the top of the water with a great *lob* or *garden worm*, or rather two ; which you are to fish for in a place where the water runs somewhat quietly (for in a stream it wil not be so well discerned.) I say, in a quiet or dead place neer to some swift, there draw your bait over the top of the water to and fro, and if there be a good *Trout* in the hole, he wil take it, especially if the night be dark ; for then he lies boldly neer the top of the water, watching the motion of any *frog* or *water-mouse*, or *rat* betwixt him and the skie, which he hunts for if he sees the water but wrinkle or move in one of these dead holes, where the great *Trouts* usually lye neer to their hold.

And you must fish for him with a strong line, and not a little hook, and let him have time to gorge your hook, for he does not usually forsake it, as he oft will in the day-fishing : and if the night be not dark, then fish so with an *artificial fly* of a light colour ; nay he will sometimes rise at a dead mouse or a piece of cloth, or any thing that seems to swim cross the water, or to be in motion : this is a choice way, but I have not oft used it because it is void of the pleasures that such dayes as these that we now injoy, afford an *angler.*

And you are to know, that in *Hampshire*, (which I think exceeds all *England* for pleasant brooks, and store of *Trouts*) they use to catch *Trouts* in the night by the light of a torch or straw, which when they have discovered, they strike with a *Trout* spear : this kind of way they catch many, but I would not believe it till I was an eye-witness of it, nor like it now I have seen it.

Viat. But master, do not *Trouts* see us in the night ?

Pisc. Yes, and hear, and smel too, both then and in the

day time, for *Gesner* observes, the *Otter* smels a fish forty furlongs off him in the water; and that it may be true, is affirmed by Sir *Francis Bacon* (in the eighth century of his natural history) who there proves, that waters may be the *Medium* of sounds, by demonstrating it thus, *that if you knock two stones together very deep under the water, those that stand on a bank neer to that place may hear the noise without any diminution of it by the water.* He also offers the like experiment concerning the letting an *Anchor* fall by a very long cable or rope on a rock, or the sand within the sea: and this being so wel observed and demonstrated, as it is by that learned man, has made me to believe that eeles unbed themselves, and stir at the noise of the thunder, and not only as some think, by the motion or the stirring of the earth, which is occasioned by that Thunder.

And this reason of Sir *Francis Bacons* [*] has made me crave pardoned of one that I laughed at, for affirming that he knew *Carps* come to a certain place in a pond to be fed at the ringing of a bel: and it shall be a rule for me to make as little noise as I can when I am fishing, until Sir *Francis Bacon* be confuted, which I shal give any man leave to do, and so leave off this philosophical discourse for a discourse of fishing.

Of which my next shall be to tell you, it is certain, that certain fields neer *Lemster*, a town in *Herefordshire*, are observed, that they make the sheep that graze upon them more fat than the next, and also to bear finer wool; that is to say, that that year in which they feed in such a particular pasture, they shall yeeld finer wool than the yeer before they came to feed in it, and coarser again if they shall return to their former pasture, and again return to a finer wool being fed in the fine wool ground. Which I tell you, that you may the better believe that I am certain, if I catch a *Trout* in one meadow, he shall be *white* and *faint*, and very like to be *lowsie;* and as certainly if I catch a *Trout* in the next meadow, he shal be *strong*, and *red*, and *lusty*, and much better meat: Trust me (scholer) I have caught many a *Trout* in a particular

[*] *Exper. 792.*

meadow, that the very shape and inamelled colour of him, has joyed me to look upon him, and I have with *Solomon* concluded, *every thing is beautifull in his season.*

It is now time to tell you next, (according to promise) some observations of the *Salmon;* but first, I will tel you there is a fish, called by some an *Umber,* and by some a *Greyling,* a choice fish, esteemed by many to be equally good with the *Trout:* it is a fish that is usually about eighteen inches long, he lives in such streams as the *Trout* does; and is indeed taken with the same bait as a *Trout* is, for he will bite both at the *minnow,* the *worm,* and the *fly,* both *natural* and *artificial:* of this fish there be many in *Trent,* and in the river that runs by *Salisbury,* and in some other lesser brooks; but he is not so general a fish as the *Trout* is; of which two fishes I will now take my leave, and come to my promised observations of the *Salmon,* and a little advice for the catching him.

CHAP. VI.

THE *Salmon* is ever bred in the fresh rivers (and in most rivers about the month of *August*) and never grows big but in the *sea;* and there to an incredible bigness in a very short time; to which place they covet to swim, by the instinct of nature, about a set time: but if they be stopp'd by *mills, floud-gates* or *weirs,* or be by accident lost in the fresh water, when the others go (which is usually by flocks or sholes) then they thrive not.

And the old *Salmon,* both the *melter* and *spawner,* strive also to get into the *sea* before winter; but being stopt that course, or lost, grow sick in fresh waters, and by degrees unseasonable, and kipper, that is, to have a bony gristle, to grow (not unlike a *hauks* beak) on one of his chaps, which hinders him from feeding, and then he pines and dies.

But if he goes to *sea,* then that gristle wears away, or is cast off (as the *eagle* is said to cast his bill) and he recovers his strength, and comes next summer to the same river, (if it be possible) to enjoy the former pleasures that there possest him ; for (as one has wittily observed) he has (like some persons of honour and riches, which have both their winter and summer houses, the fresh rivers for summer, and the salt water for winter to spend his life in ; which is not (as Sir *Francis Bacon* hath observed *) above ten years : and it is to be observed, that though they grow big in the *sea*, yet they grow not fat but in fresh rivers ; and it is observed, that the farther they get from the *sea*, the better they be.

And it is observed, that, to the end they may get far from the *sea*, either to spawne or to possess the pleasure that they then and there find, they will force themselves over the tops of *weirs*, or *hedges*, or *stops* in the water, by taking their tails into their mouthes, and leaping over those places, even to a height beyond common belief : and sometimes by forcing themselves against the streame through sluces and floud-gates, beyond common credit. And 'tis observed by *Gesner*, that there is none bigger than in *England*, nor none better than in Thames.

And for the *Salmons* sudden growth, it has been observed by tying a ribbon in the tail of some number of the young *Salmons*, which have been taken in *weires*, as they swimm'd towards the salt water, and then by taking a part of them again with the same mark, at the same place, at their returne from the sea, which is usually about six months after; and the like experiment hath been tried upon young *swallows*, who have after six months absence, been observed to return to the same chimney, there to make their nests and their habitations for the summer following; which hath inclined many to think, that every *Salmon* usually returns to the same river in which it was bred, as young *pigeons* taken out the same *dove-cote*, have also been observed to do.

And you are yet to observe further, that the He *Salmon* is usually bigger than the spawner, and that he is more kipper, and less able to endure a winter in the fresh water, then the She is ; yet she is at that time of looking less kipper and better, as watry and as bad meat.

* In his History of Life and Death.

And yet you are to observe, that as there is no general rule without an exception, so there are some few rivers in this nation that have *Trouts* and *Salmon* in season in winter. But for the observation of that and many other things, I must in manners omit, because they will prove too large for our narrow compass of time, and therefore I shall next fall upon my direction how to fish for the *Salmon.*

And for that, first, you shall observe, that usually he staies not long in a place (as *Trouts* wil) but (as I said) covets still to go neerer the spring head ; and that he does not (as the *Trout* and many other fish) lie neer the water side or bank, or roots of trees, but swims usually in the middle, and neer the ground ; and that there you are to fish for him ; and that he is to be caught as the *Trout* is, with a *worm,* a *minnow,* (which some call a *penke*) or with a *fly.*

And you are to observe that he is very, very seldom observed to bite at a *minnow* (yet sometimes he will) and not oft at a *fly,* but more usually at a *worm,* and then most usually at a *lob* or *garden worm,* which should be well scowred, that is to say, seven or eight dayes in moss before you fish with them ; and if you double your time of eight into sixteen, or more, into twenty or more days, it is still the better, for the worms will stil be clearer, tougher, and more lively, and continue so longer upon your hook.

And now I shall tell you, that which may be called a secret : I have been a fishing with old *Oliver Henly* (now with God) a noted fisher, both for *Trout* and *Salmon,* and have observed that he would usually take three or four worms out of his bag and put them into a little box in his pocket, where he would usually let them continue half an hour or more, before he would bait his hook with them ; I have ask'd him his reason, and he has replied, *he did but pick the best out to be in a readiness against he baited his hook the next time:* but he has been observed both by others, and my self, to catch more fish than I or any other body, that has ever gone a fishing with him, could do, especially *Salmons;* and I have been told lately by one of his most intimate and secret friends, that the box in which he put those worms was anointed with a drop, or two, or three of the oil of *ivyberries*, made by expression or infusion, and that by the wormes remaining in that box an hour, or a like time, they had incorporated a kind of smel that was irresistibly attractive, enough to force any fish, within the smel of them, to bite. This I heard not long since from a friend, but have not tryed it ; yet I grant it probable, and refer my reader to Sir *Francis Bacons* natural history, where he proves fishes may hear ; and I am certain *Gesner* sayes, the *Otter* can smell in the water, and know not but that fish may do so too : 'tis left for a lover of angling, or any that desires to improve that art, to try this conclusion.

I shall also impart another experiment (but not tryed by my selfe) which I will deliver in the same words as it was by a friend, given me in writing.

Take the stinking oil drawn out of polypody of the oak, by a retort mixt with turpentine, and hive-honey, and annoint your bait therewith, and it will doubtlesse draw the fish to it.

But in these things I have no great faith, yet grant it probable, and have had from some chymical men (namely, Sir *George Hastings* and others) an affirmation of them to be very advantageous : but no more of these, especially not in this place.

I might here, before I take my leave of the *Salmon*, tell you, that there is more than one sort of them, as namely, a *Tecon*, and another called in some places a *Samlet*, or by some a *Skegger:* but these (and others which I forbear to name) may be fish of another kind, and differ, as we know a *Herring* and a *Pilcher* do ; but must by me be left to the disquisitions of men of more leisure and of greater abilities, then I profess myself to have.

And lastly, I am to borrow so much of your promised patience, as to tell you, that the *Trout* or *Salmon*, being in season, have at their first taking out of the water (which continues during life) their bodies adorned, the one with such red spots, and the other with black or blackish spots, which gives them such an addition of natural beautie, as I (that yet am no enemy to it) think was never given to any woman by the artificial paint or patches in which they so much pride themselves in this age. And so I shall leave them and proceed to some observations of the *Pike.*

CHAP. VII.

Pisc. IT is not to be doubted but that the *Luce,* or *Pikrell,* or *Pike* breeds by spawning ; and yet *Gesner* sayes, that some of them breed, where none ever was, out of a weed called *Pikrell-weed,* and other glutinous matter, which withe help of the suns heat proves in some particular ponds (apted by nature for it) to become *Pikes.*

Sir *Francis Bacon** observes the *Pike* to be the longest lived of any fresh water fish, and yet that his life is not usually above fortie years ; and yet *Gesner* mentions a *Pike* taken in *Swedeland* in the year 1449, with a ring about his neck, declaring he was put into the pond by *Frederick* the second, more than two hundred years before he was last taken, as the inscription of that ring, being Greek, was interpreted by the then Bishop of *Worms.* But of this no more, but that it is observed that the old or very great *Pikes* have in them more of state than goodness ; the smaller or middle siz'd *Pikes* being by the most and choicest palates observed to be the best meat ; but contrary, the Eele is observed to be the better for age and bigness.

All *Pikes* that live long prove chargeable to their keepers, because their life is maintained by the death of so many other fish, even those of his owne kind, which has made him by some writers to be called the *tyrant* of the rivers, or the *fresh-water wolf,* by reason of his bold, greedy, devouring disposition ; which is so keen, as *Gesner* relates, a man going to a pond (where it seems a *Pike* had devoured all the fish) to water his mule, had a *Pike* bit his mule by the lips, to which the *Pike* hung so fast, that the *mule* drew him out of the water, and by that accident the owner

---

* In his History of Life and Death.

of the *mule* got the *Pike;* I tell you who relates it, and shall with it tel you what a wise man has observed, *it is a hard thing to perswade the belly, because it hath no ears.*

But if this relation of *Gesners* bee disbelieved, it is too evident to bee doubted that a *Pike* will devoure a fish of his own kind, that shall be bigger than this belly or throat will receive ; and swallow a part of him, and let the other part remaine in his mouth till the swallowed part be digested, and then swallow that other part that was in his mouth, and so put it over by degrees. And it is observed, that the *Pike* will eat venemous things (as some kind of *frogs* are) and yet live without being harmed by them : for, as some say, he has in him a natural balsome or antidote against all poison : and others, that he never eats a venemous *frog* till he hath first killed her, and then (as *ducks* are observed to do to *frogs* in spawning time, at which time some *frogs* are observed to be venemous) so throughly washt her, by tumbling her up and down in the water, that he may devour her without danger. And *Gesner* affirms, that a *Polonian* gentleman did faithfully assure him, he had seen two young geese at one time in the belly of a *Pike :* and hee observes, that in *Spain* there are no *Pikes*, and that the biggest are in the lake *Thracimane* in *Italy*, and the next, if not equal to them, are the *Pikes* of *England.*

The *Pike* is also observed to be a melancholly, and a bold fish : melancholly, because he alwaies swims or rests himselfe alone, and never swims in sholes, or with company, as *Roach*, and *Dace*, and most other fish do : and bold, because he fears not a shadow, or to see or be seen of any body, as the *Trout* and *Chub*, and all other fish do.

And it is observed by *Gesner*, that the bones, and hearts, and gals of *Pikes* are very medicinable for several diseases, as to stop bloud, to abate fevers, to cure agues, to oppose or expel the infections of the plague, and to be many wayes medicinable and useful for the good of mankind ; but that the biting of a *Pike* is venemous and hard to be cured.

And it is observed, that the *Pike* is a fish that breeds.

5—2

but once a year, and that other fish (as namely *Loaches*)·
do breed oftner; as we are certain pigeons do almost
every month, and yet the hawk, a bird of prey (as the
Pike is of fish) breeds but once in twelve months; and
you are to note, that his time of breeding or spawning is
usually about the end of *February;* or somewhat later, in
March, as the weather proves colder or warmer : and to
note, that his manner of breeding is thus, a he and a she
Pike will usually go together out of a river into some ditch
or creek, and that there the spawner casts her eggs, and the
melter hovers over her all that time that she is casting her
spawn, but touches her not. I might say more of this,
but it might be thought curiosity or worse, and shall therefore forbear it, and take up so much of your attention as
to tell you, that the best of *Pikes* are noted to be in rivers,
then those in great ponds or meres, and the worst in smal
ponds.

And now I shall proceed to give you some directions
how to catch this *Pike* which you have with so much patience heard me talk of.

His feeding is usually fish or frogs, and sometimes a
weed of his owne, called *pikrel-weed*, of which I told you
some think some Pikes are bred; for they have observed,
that where no pikes have been put into a pond, yet that
there they have been found, and that there has been
plenty of that weed in that pond, and that that weed both
breeds and feeds them; but whether those *Pikes* so bred
will ever breed by generation as the others do, I shall
leave to the disquisitions of men of more curiosity and
leisure than I profess my self to have; and shall proceed
to tell you, that you may fish for a *Pike*, either with a
ledger, or a walking bait; and you are to note, that I call
that a ledger which is fix'd, or made to rest in one certaine
place when you shall be absent; and that I call that a
walking bait, which you take with you, and have ever in
motion. Concerning which two, I shall give you this
direction, that your ledger bait is best to be a living bait,
whether it be a fish or a frog; and that you may make
them live the longer, you may, or indeed you must take
this course :

First, for your live bait of fish, a *Roch* or *Dace* is (I think) best and most tempting, and a *Pearch* the longest liv'd on a hook; you must take your knife, (which cannot be too sharp) and betwixt the head and the fin on his back, cut or make an insition, or such a scar as you may put the arming wyer of your hook into it, with as little bruising or hurting the fish as art and diligence will enable you to do, and so carrying your arming wyer along his back, unto, or neer the tail of your fish, betwixt the skin and the body of it, draw out that wyer or arming of your hook at another scar neer to his tail ; then tye him about it with thred, but no harder then of necessitie you must to prevent hurting the fish ; and the better to avoid hurting the fish, some have a kind of probe to open the way, for the more easie entrance and passage of your wyer or arming : but as for these, time and a little experience will teach you better then I can by words ; for of this I will for the present say no more, but come next to give you some directions how to bait your hook with a frog.

Viat. But, good master, did not you say even now, that same *frogs* were venemous, and is it not dangerous to touch them ?

Pisc. Yes, but I wil give you some rules or cautions concerning them : and first, you are to note, there is two kinds of *frogs;* that is to say, (if I may so express my self) a *flesh* and a *fish-frog :* by flesh *frogs*, I mean, *frogs* that breed and live on the land ; and of these there be several sorts and colours, some being peckled, some greenish, some blackish, or brown : the green *frog*, which is a smal one, is by *Topsell* taken to be venemous ; and so is the *padock*, or *frog-padock*, which usually keeps or breeds on the land, and is very large and bony, and big, especially the She *frog* of that kind ; yet these will sometime come into the water, but it is not often ; and the land *frogs* are some of them observed by him, to breed by laying eggs, and others to breed of the slime and dust of the earth, and that in winter they turn to slime again, and that the next summer that very slime returns to be a living creature ; this is the opinion of *Pliny :* and * *Cardanus* undertakes

* In his 16th Book, *De subtil. ex.*

to give reason for the raining of *frogs;* but if it were in my power, it should rain none but water *frogs*, for those I think are not venomous, especially the right water *frog*, which about *February* or *March* breeds in ditches by slime and blackish eggs in that slime, about which time of breeding the He and She *frog* are observed to use divers simber salts, and to croke and make a noise, which the land *frog*, or *padock frog* never does. Now of these water *frogs*, you are to chuse the yellowest that you can get, for that the *Pike* ever likes best. And thus use your *frog*, that he may continue long alive :

Put your hook into his mouth, which you may easily do from about the middle of *April* till *August*, and then the *frogs* mouth grows up and he continues so for at least six months without eating, but is sustained, none, but he whose name is Wonderful, knows how. I say, put your hook, I mean the arming wire, though his mouth and out at his gills, and then with a fine needle and silk sow the upper part of his leg with only one stitch to the armed wire of your hook, or tie the *frogs* leg above the upper joint to the armed wire, and in so doing use him as though you loved him, that is, harme him as little as you may possibly, that he may live the longer.

And now, having given you this direction for the baiting your ledger hook with a live fish or frog, my next must be to tell you, how your hook thus baited must or may be used ; and it is thus : having fastned your hook to a line, which if it be not fourteen yards long, should not be less than twelve ; you are to fasten that line to any bow neer to a hole where a *Pike* is, or is likely to lye, or to have a haunt, and then wind your line on any forked stick, all your line, except a half yard of it, or rather more, and split that forked stick with such a nick or notch at one end of it, as may keep the line from any more of it ravelling from about the stick, than so much of it as you intended ; and chuse your forked stick to be of that bigness as may keep the *fish* or *frog* from pulling the forked stick under the water till the *Pike* bites, and then the *Pike* having pulled the line forth of the clift or nick in which it was gently fastened, will have line enough to go to his hold and powch the bait : and if you would have this ledger bait to keep at a fixt place, undisturbed by wind or other accidents, which may drive it to the shoare side (for you are to note that it is likeliest to catch a *Pike* in the midst of the water) then hang a small plummet of lead, a stone, or piece of tyle, or a turfe in a string, and caste it into the water, with the forked stick to hang upon the ground, to be as an anchor to keep the forked stick from moving out of your intended place till the *Pike* come. This I take to be a very good way, to use so many ledger baits as you intend to make tryal of.

Or if you bait your hooks thus, with live fish or frogs, and in a windy day fasten them thus to a bow or bundle of straw, and by the help of that wind can get them to move cross a *pond* or *mere*, you are like to stand still on the shoar and see sport, if there be any store of *Pikes ;* or these live baits may make sport, being tied about the body or wings of a *goose* or *duck*, and she chased over a pond : and the like may be done with turning three or four live baits thus fastned to bladders, or boughs, or bottles of hay, or flags, to swim down a *river*, whilst you walk quietly on the shore along with them, and are still in expectation of sport. The rest must be taught you by practice, for time will not alow me to say more of this kind of fishing with live baits.

And for your dead bait for a *Pike*, for that you may be taught by one dayes going a fishing with me or any other body that fishes for him, for the baiting your hook with a dead *Gudgion* or a *Roch*, and moving it up and down the water, is too easie a thing to take up any time to direct you to do it ; and yet, because I cut you short in that, I will commute for it, by telling you that that was told me for a secret : it is this :

Dissolve gum of ivie *in oyle of* spike, *and therewith annoint your dead bait for a* Pike, *and then cast it into a likely place, and when it has layen a short time at the bottom, draw it towards the top of the water, and so up the stream, and it is more than likely that you have a* Pike *follow you with more than common eagerness.*

This has not been tryed by me, but told me by a friend

of note, that pretended to do me a courtesie : but if this
direction to catch a Pike thus do you no good, I am certaine this direction how to roste him when he is caught,
is choicely good, for I have tried it, and it is somewhat
the better for not being common ; but with my direction
you must take this caution, that your Pike must not be a
smal one.

First, open your Pike *at the gills, and if need be, cut
also a little slit towards his belly; out of these, take his
guts, and keep his liver, which you are to shred very
small with* time, sweet margerom, *and a little* winter-
savoury ; *to these put some pickled* oysters, *and some* anchovis, *both these last whole (for the* anchovis *will melt,
and the* oysters *should not) to these you must add also a
pound of sweet butter, which you are to mix with the
herbs that are shred, and let them all be well salted (if
the* Pike *be more than a yard long, then you may put into
these herbs more than a pound, or if he be less, then less
butter will suffice :) these being thus mixt, with a blade or
two of mace, must be put into the* Pikes *belly, and then his
belly sowed up; then you are to thrust the spit through
his mouth out at his tail; and then with four, or five, or
six split sticks or very thin laths, and a convenient quantitie of tape or filiting, these laths are to be tyed round
the* Pikes *body, from his head to his tail, and the tape tied
somewhat thick to prevent his breaking or falling off
from the spit; let him be roasted very leisurely, and often
basted with claret wine, and anchovis, and butter mixt
together, and also with what moisture falls from him
into the pan : when you have rosted him sufficiently, you
are to hold under him (when you unwind or cut the tape
that ties him) such a dish as you purpose to eat him out
of, and let him fall into it with the sawce that is rosted
in his belly; and by this means the* Pike *will be kept un-
broken and complete; then to the sawce, which was within
him, and also in the pan, you are to add a fit quantity of
the best butter, and to squeeze the juice of three or four
oranges : lastly, you may either put into the* Pike *with the*
oysters, *two cloves of garlick, and take it whole out when
the* Pike *is cut off the spit, or to give the sawce a hogoe,*

let the dish (into which you let the Pike *fall) be rubed with it; the using or not using of this garlick is left to your discretion.*

This dish of meat is too good for any but anglers or honest men ; and, I trust, you wil prove both, therefore I have trusted you with this secret. And now I shall proceed to give you some observations concerning the *Carp*.

~~~~~~~~~~~~~~~

CHAP. VIII.

Pisc. THE *Carp* is a stately, a good, and a subtle fish, a fish that hath not (as it is said) been long in *England*, but said to be by one Mr. *Mascall* (a gentleman then living at *Plumsted* in *Sussex*) brought into this nation : and for the better confirmation of this, you are to remember I told you that *Gesner* sayes, there is not a *Pike* in *Spain*, and that except the Eele, which lives longest out of the water, there is none that will endure more hardness, or live longer than a *Carp* will out of it, and so the report of his being brought out of a forrain nation into this, is the more probable.

Carps and *Loches* are observed to breed several months in one year, which most other fish do not, and it is the rather believed, because you shall scarce or never take a *Male Carp* without a *melt*, or a *Female* without a *roe* or *spawn;* and for the most part very much, and especially all the summer season ; and it is observed, that they breed more naturally in ponds than in running waters, and that those that live in rivers are taken by men of the best palates to be much the better meat.

And it is observed, that in some ponds *Carps* will not breed, especially in cold ponds ; but where they will breed, they breed innumerably, if there be no *Pikes* nor *Pearch* to devour their spawn, when it is cast upon grass, or flags, or weeds, where it lies ten or twelve dayes before it be enlivened.

The *Carp*, if he have water room and good feed, will

grow to a very great bigness and length : I have heard to above a yard long ; though I never saw one above thirty three inches, which was a very great and goodly fish.

Now as the increase of *Carps* is wonderful for their number ; so there is not a reason found out, I think, by any, why they should breed in some ponds, and not in others of the same nature, for soil and all other circumstances ; and as their breeding, so are their decayes also very mysterious ; I have both read it, and been told by a gentleman of tryed honestie, that he has knowne sixtie or more large *Carps* put into several ponds neer to a house, where by reason of the stakes in the ponds, and the owners constant being neer to them, it was impossible they should be stole away from him, and that when he has after three or four years emptied the pond, and expected an increase from them by breeding young ones. (for that they might do so, he had, as the rule is, put in three melters for one spawner) he has, I say, after three or four years found neither a young nor old *Carp* remaining : and the like I have known of one that has almost watched his pond, and at a like distance of time at the fishing of a pond, found of seventy or eighty large *Carps*, not above five or six : and that he had forborn longer to fish the said pond, but that he saw in a hot day in summer, a large *Carp* swim neer to the top of the water with a *frog* upon his head, and that he upon that occasion caused his pond to be let dry : and I say, of seventy or eighty *Carps*, only found five or six in the said pond, and those very sick and lean, and with every one a frog sticking so fast on the head of the said *Carps*, that the frog would not bee got off without extreme force or killing, and the gentleman that did affirm this to me, told me he saw it, and did declare his belief to be (and I also believe the same) that he thought the other *Carps* that were so strangely lost, were so killed by *frogs*, and then devoured.

But I am faln into this discourse by accident, of which I might say more, but it has proved longer than I intended, and possibly may not to you be considerable ; I shall therefore give you three or four more short observations

b, and then fall upon some directions how you
or him.

: of *Carps* is by S^r. *Francis Bacon* (in his his-
: and death) observed to be but ten years; yet
hk they live longer: but most conclude, that
:o the *Pike* or *Luce*) all *Carps* are the better for
)gness; the tongues of *Carps* are noted to be
' costly meat, especially to them that buy them;
' sayes, *Carps* have no tongues like other fish,
' of flesh-like-fish in their mouth like to a tongue,
'e so called, but it is certain it is choicely good,
'e *Carp* is to be reckoned amongst those leather
ish, which I told you have their teeth in their
d for that reason he is very seldom lost by
'is hold, if your hook bee once stuck into his

'u, that Sir *Francis Bacon* thinks that the *Carp*
'n years; but *Janus Dubravius* (a *Germane* as
's writ a book in Latine of fish and fish ponds,
'? sayes, that *Carps* begin to spawn at the age
'rs, and continue to do so till thirty; he sayes
'i the time of their breeding, which is in summer
'jn hath warmed both the earth and water, and
em also for generation, that then three or four
'? will follow a female, and that then she putting
on a seeming coyness, they force her through weeds and
flags, where she lets fall her eggs or spawn, which sticks
fast to the weeds, and then they let fall their melt upon it,
and so it becomes in a short time to be a living fish; and,
as I told you, it is thought the *Carp* does this several
months in the yeer, and most believe that most she breed
after this manner, except the *Eele:* and it is thought that
all *Carps* are not bred by generation, but that some breed
otherwayes, as some *Pikes* do.

Much more might be said out of him, and out of *Aristotle,* which *Dubravius* often quotes in his discourse, but
it might rather perplex than satisfie you, and therefore I
shall rather chuse to direct you how to catch, than spend
more time in discoursing either of the nature or the
breeding of this *Carp,* or of any more circumstances con-

cerning him, but yet I shall remember you of what I told
you before, that he is a very subtle fish and hard to be
caught.

And my first direction is, that if you will fish for a *Carp*,
you must put in a very large measure of *patience*, especially to fish for a *river carp :* I have knowne a very good
fisher angle diligently four or six hours in a day, for three
or four dayes together for a *river Carp*, and not have a
bite : and you are to note, that in some ponds it is as hard
to catch a *Carp* as in a river ; that is to say, where they
have store of feed, and the water is of a clayish colour ;
but you are to remember, that I have told you there is no
rule without an exception, and therefore being possest with
that hope and patience which I wish to all fishers, especially to the *Carp-Angler*, I shall tell you with what bait
to fish for him ; but that must be either early or late, and
let me tell you, that in hot weather (for he will seldom bite
in cold) you cannot be too early or too late at it.

The *Carp* bites either at wormes or at paste ; and of
worms I think the blewish marsh or meadow worm is best ;
but possibly another worm not too big may do as well,
and so may a gentle ; and as for pastes, there are almost
as many sorts as there are medicines for the tooth-ach,
but doubtless sweet pastes are best ; I mean, pastes mixt
with honey, or with sugar ; which, that you may the better
beguile this crafty fish, should be thrown into the pond or
place in which you fish for him some hours before you
undertake your trial of skil by the angle-rod : and doubtless, if it be thrown into the water a day or two before, at
several times, and in smal pellets, you are the likelier when
you fish for the *Carp*, to obtain your desired sport : or in
a large pond, to draw them to any certain place, that they
may the better and with more hope be fished for ; you are
to throw into it, in some certaine place, either grains, or
bloud mixt with cow-dung, or with bran ; or any garbage,
as chickens guts or the like, and then some of your smal
sweet pellets, with which you purpose to angle ; these smal
pellets, being few of them thrown in as you are angling.

And your paste must bee thus made : take the flesh of
a rabet or cat cut smal, and bean-flower, or (if not easily got

then) other flowre, and then mix these together, and put to them either sugar, or honey, which I think better, and then beat these together in a mortar; or sometimes work them in your hands, (your hands being very clean) and then make it into a ball, or two, or three, as you like best for your use: but you must work or pound it so long in the mortar, as to make it so tough as to hang upon your hook without washing from it, yet not too hard; or that you may the better keep it on your hook, you may kneade with your paste a little (and not much) white or yellowish wool.

And if you would have this paste keep all the year for any other fish, then mix with it *Virgins-wax* and *clarified honey*, and work them together with your hands before the fire; then make these into balls, and it will keep all the yeer.

And if you fish for a *Carp* with gentles, then put upon your hook a small piece of scarlet about this bigness ▉, it being soked in, or annointed with *oyl of Peter*, called by some, *oyl of the rock;* and if your gentles be put two or three dayes before into a box or horn annointed with honey, and so put upon your hook, as to preserve them to be living, you are as like to kill this craftie fish this way as any other; but still as you are fishing, chaw a little white or brown bread in your mouth, and cast it into the pond about the place where your flote swims. Other baits there be, but these with diligence, and patient watchfulness, will do it as well as any as I have ever practised, or heard of: and yet I shall tell you, that the crumbs of white bread and honey made into a paste, is a good bait for a *Carp*, and you know it is more easily made. And having said thus much of the *Carp*, my next discourse shall be of the *Bream*, which shall not prove so tedious, and therefore I desire the continuance of your attention.

CHAP. IX.

Pisc. THE *Bream* being at a full growth, is a large and stately fish, he will breed both in rivers and ponds, but loves best to live in ponds, where, if he likes the aire, he will grow not only to be very large, but as'fat as a hog : he is by *Gesner* taken to be more pleasant or sweet than wholesome ; this fish is long in growing, but breeds exceedingly in a water that pleases him, yea, in many ponds so fast, as to over store them, and starve the other fish.

The baits good for to catch the *Bream* are many ; as namely, young wasps, and a paste made of brown bread and honey, or gentles, or especially a worm, a worm that is not much unlike a magot, which you will find at the roots of *docks,* or of *flags,* or of *rushes* that grow in the water, or watry places, and a *grashopper* having his legs nip'd off, or a flye that is in *June* and *July* to be found amongst the green reed, growing by the water side, those are said to bee excellent baits. I doubt not but there be many others that both the *Bream* and the *Carp* also would bite at ; but these time and experience will teach you how to find out : and so having according to my promise given you these short observations concerning the *Bream,* I shall also give you some observations concerning the *Tench,* and those also very briefly.

The *Tench* is observed to love to live in ponds : but if he be in a river, then in the still places of the river, he is observed to be a physician to other fishes, and is so called by many that have been searchers into the nature of fish ; and it is said, that a *Pike* will neither devour nor hurt him, because the *Pike* being sick or hurt by any accident, is cured by touching the *Tench,* and the *Tench* does the like to other fishes, either by touching them, or by being in their company.

Randelitius sayes in his discourse of fishes (quoted by *Gesner*) that at his being at *Rome,* he saw certaine Jewes apply *Tenches* to the feet of a sick man for a cure ; and it is observed, that many of those people have many secrets unknown to Christians, secrets which have never been

written, but have been successively since the dayes of
Solomon (who knew the nature of all things from the
shrub to the cedar) delivered by tradition from the father
to the son, and so from generation to generation without
writing, or (unless it were casually) without the least com-
municating them to any other nation or tribe (for to do so,
they account a profanation) : yet this fish, that does by a
natural inbred balsome, not only cure himselfe if he be
wounded, but others also, loves not to live in clear streams
paved with gravel, but in standing waters, where mud and
the worst of weeds abound, and therefore it is, I think,
that this *Tench* is by so many accounted better for medicines than for meat : but for the first, I am able to say
little; and for the later, can say positively, that he eats
pleasantly; and will therefore give you a few, and but a
few directions how to catch him.

He will bite at a paste made of brown bread and honey,
or at a marsh-worm, or a lob-worm; he will bite also at a
smaller worm, with his head nip'd off, and a cod-worm put
on the hook before the worm; and I doubt not but that
he will, also in the three hot months (for in the nine colder
he stirs not much) bite at a flag-worm, or at a green gentle,
but can positively say no more of the *Tench*, he being a
fish that I have not often angled for; but I wish my
honest scholer may, and be ever fortunate when hee fishes.

Viat. I thank you good master : but I pray sir, since
you see it still rains *May*butter, give me some observations
and directions concerning the *Pearch*, for they say he is
both a very good and a bold biting fish, and I would fain
learne to fish for him.

Pisc. You say true, scholer, the *Pearch* is a very good,
and a very bold biting fish, he is one of the fishes of prey,
that, like the *Pike* and *Trout*, carries his teeth in his
mouth, not in his throat, and dare venture to kill and
devour another fish; this fish, and the *Pike* are (sayes
Gesner) the best of fresh water fish; he spawns but once
a year, and is by physicians held very nutritive; yet by
many to be hard of digestion : they abound more in the
river *Poe*, and in *England*, (sayes *Randelitius*) than other
parts, and have in their brain a stone, which is in forrain

parts sold by apothecaries, being there noted to be very medicinable against the stone in the reins : these be a part of the commendations which some philosophycal brains have bestowed upon the fresh-water *Pearch*, yet they commend the sea *Pearch*, which is known by having but one fin on his back, (of which they say, we *English* see but a few) to be a much better fish.

The *Pearch* grows slowly, yet will grow, as I have been credibly informed, to be almost two foot long ; for my informer told me, such a one was not long since taken by Sir *Abraham Williams*, a gentleman of worth, and a lover of angling, that yet lives, and I wish he may : this was a deep bodied fish ; and doubtless durst have devoured a *Pike* of half his own length ; for I have told you, he is a bold fish, such a one, as but for extreme hunger, the *Pike* will not devour ; for to affright the *Pike*, the *Pearch* will set up his fins, much like as a *Turkie-cock* wil sometimes set up his tail.

But, my scholer, the *Pearch* is not only valiant to defend himself, but he is (as you said) a bold biting fish, yet he will not bite at all seasons of the yeer ; he is very abstemious in winter ; and hath been observed by some, not usually to bite till the *mulberry tree* buds, that is to say, till extreme frosts be past for that spring ; for when the *mulberry tree* blossomes, many gardners observe their forward fruit to be past the danger of frosts, and some have made the like observation of the *Pearches* biting.

But bite the Pearch will, and that very boldly ; and as one has wittily observed, if there be twentie or fortie in a hole, they may be at one standing all catch'd one after another ; they being, as he saies, like the wicked of the world, not afraid though their fellowes and companions perish in their sight.

And the baits for this bold fish are not many ; I mean, he will bite as well at some, or at any of these three, as at any or all others whatsoever ; a *worm*, a *minnow*, or a little *frog* (of which you may find many in hay time) and of *worms*, the dunghill worm, called a *brandling*, I take to be best, being well scowred in moss or fennel ; and if you fish for a *Pearch* with a *minnow*, then it is best to be alive, you sticking your hook through his back fin, and letting him swim up and down about mid-water, or a little lower, and you still keeping him to about that depth, by a cork, which ought not to be a very light one : and the like way you are to fish for the *Pearch* with a small *frog*, your hook being fastened through the skin of his leg, towards the upper part of it : and lastly, I will give you but this advise, that you give the *Pearch* time enough when he bites, for there was scarse ever any *angler* that has given him too much. And now I think best to rest my selfe, for I have almost spent my spirits with talking so long.

Viat. Nay, good master, one fish more, for you see it rains still, and you know our angles are like money put to usury ; they may thrive though we sit still and do nothing, but talk and enjoy one another. Come, come the other fish, good master.

Pisc. But scholer, have you nothing to mix with this discourse, which now grows both tedious and tiresome ? shall I have nothing from you that seems to have both a good memorie, and a chearful spirit ?

Viat. Yes, master, I will speak you a coppie of verses that were made by Doctor *Donne*, and made to shew the world that hee could make soft and smooth verses, when he thought them fit and worth his labour ; and I love them the better, because they allude to rivers, and fish, and fishing. They be these :

> Come live with me, and be my love,
> And we will some new pleasures prove,
> Of golden sands and christal brooks,
> With silken lines and silver hooks.
>
> There will the river whispering run,
> Warm'd by the eyes more than the sun ;
> And there th' inamel'd fish wil stay,
> Begging themselves they may betray.
>
> When thou wilt swim in that live bath,
> Each fish, which every channel hath
> Most amorously to thee will swim,
> Gladder to catch thee than thou him.

6

If thou to be so seen beest loath,
By sun or moon, thou darknest both ;
And, if mine eyes have leave to see,
I need not their light, having thee.

Let others freeze with angling reeds,
And cut their legs with shels and weeds,
Or treacherously poor fish beset,
With strangling snares, or windowy net.

Let coarse bold hands, from slimy nest,
The bedded fish in banks outwrest,
Let curious traitors sleave silk flies,
To 'witch poor wandring fishes eyes.

For thee thou needst no such deceit,
For thou thy self art thine own bait ;
That fish that is not catch'd thereby,
Is wiser far, alas, than I.

Pisc. Well remembred, honest scholer, I thank you for
these choice verses, which I have heard formerly, but had
quite forgot, till they were recovered by your happie
memorie. Well, being I have now rested my self a little,
I will make you some requital, by telling you some observations of the *Eele,* for it rains still, and (as you say) our
angles are as money put to use, that thrive when we play.

CHAP. X.

IT is agreed by most men, that the *Eele* is both a good
and a most daintie fish ; but most men differ about his
breeding ; some say, they breed by generation as other
fish do ; and others, that they breed (as some worms do)
out of the putrefaction of the earth, and divers other waies ;
those that denie them to breed by generation, as other fish
do, ask, if any man ever saw an *Eel* to have spawn or
melt ? and they are answered, that they may be as certain
of their breeding, as if they had seen spawn ; for they say,
that they are certain that *Eeles* have all parts fit for generation, like other fish, but so smal as not to be easily dis-

cerned, by reason of their fatness ; but that discerned they may be ; and that the Hee and the She *Eele* may be distinguished by their fins.

And others say, that *Eeles* growing old, breed other *Eeles* out of the corruption of their own age, which Sir *Francis Bacon* sayes, exceeds not ten years. And others say, that *Eeles* are bred of a particular dew falling in the months of *May* or *June* on the banks of some particular ponds or rivers (apted by nature for that end) which in a few dayes is by the suns heat turned into *Eeles*. I have seen in the beginning of *July*, in a river not far from *Canterbury*, some parts of it covered over with young *Eeles* about the thickness of a straw ; and these *Eeles* did lye on the top of that water, as thick as motes are said to be in the sun ; and I have heard the like of other rivers, as namely in *Severn*, and in a *pond* or *mere* in *Stafford-shire*, where about a set time in summer, such small *Eeles* abound so much, that many of the poorer sort of people, that inhabit near to it, take such *Eeles* out of this mere, with sieves or sheets, and make a kind of *Eele-cake* of them, and eat it like as bread. And *Gesner* quotes venerable *Bede* to say, that in *England* there is an iland called *Ely*, by reason of the innumerable number of *Eeles* that breed in it. But that *Eeles* may be bred as some worms and some kind of *bees* and *wasps* are, either of dew, or out of the corruption of the earth, seems to be made probable by the *barnacles* and young *goslings* bred by the suns heat and the rotten planks of an old ship, and hatched of trees, both which are related for truths by *Dubartas*, and our learned *Cambden*, and laborious *Gerrard* in his *Herball.*

It is said by *Randelitius*, that those *Eeles* that are bred in rivers, that relate to, or be neer to the sea, never return to the fresh waters (as the *Salmon* does alwaies desire to do) when they have once tasted the salt water ; and I do the more easily believe this, because I am certain that powdered beef is a most excellent bait to catch an *Eele :* and Sir *Francis Bacon* will allow the *Eeles* life to be but ten years ; yet he in his history of life and death, mentions a *Lamprey* belonging to the *Roman* emperor, to be made tame, and so kept for almost three-score yeers ; and that such useful and pleasant observations were made of this *Lamprey*, that *Crassus* the oratour (who kept her) lamented her death.

It is granted by all, or most men, that *Eeles*, for about six months (that is to say, the six cold months of the yeer) stir not up and down, neither in the rivers nor the pools in which they are, but get into the soft earth or mud, and there many of them together bed themselves, and live without feeding upon any thing (as I have told you some *Swallows* have been observed to do in hollow trees for those six cold months); and this the *Eele* and *Swallow* do, as not being able to endure winter weather; for *Gesner* quotes *Albertus* to say, that in the yeer 1125 (that years winter being more cold than usual) *Eeles* did by natures instinct get out of the water into a stack of hay in a meadow upon dry ground, and there bedded themselves, but yet at last died there. I shall say no more of the *Eele*, but that, as it is observed, he is impatient of cold, so it has been observed, that in warm weather an *Eele* has been known to live five days out of the water. And lastly, let me tell you, that some curious searchers into the natures of fish, observe that there be several sorts or kinds of *Eeles*, as the *silver Eele* and green or *greenish Eele* (with which the river Thames abounds, and are called *gregs*); and a blackish *Eele*, whose head is more flat and bigger then ordinary *Eeles;* and also an *Eele* whose fins are redish, and but seldome taken in this nation (and yet taken sometimes) : these several kinds of *Eeles*, are (say some) diversly bred; as namely, out of the corruption of the earth, and by dew, and other wayes (as I have said to you :) and yet it is affirmed by some, that for a certain, the *silver Eele* breeds by generation, but not by spawning as other fish do, but that her brood come alive from her no bigger nor longer than a pin, and I have had too many testimonies of this to doubt the truth of it.

And this *Eele* of which I have said so much to you, may be caught with divers kinds of baits ; as namely, with powdered beef, with a *lob* or *garden-worm*, with a *minnow*, or gut of a *hen, chicken*, or with almost any thing, for he is a greedy fish : but the *Eele* seldome stirs in the day, but then hides himselfe, and therefore he is usually caught by night, with one of these baits of which I have spoken, and then caught by laying hooks, which you are to fasten to the bank, or twigs of a tree; or by throwing a string cross the stream, with many hooks at it, and baited with the foresaid baits, and a clod or plummet, or stone, thrown into the river with this line, that so you may in the morning find it neer to some fixt place, and then take it up with a drag-hook or otherwise : but these things are indeed too common to be spoken of; and an hours fishing with any *angler* will teach you better, both for these, and many other common things in the practical part of *angling*, than a weeks discourse. I shall therefore conclude this direction for taking the *Eele*, by telling you, that in a warm day in summer, I have taken many a good *Eele* by *snigling*, and have been much pleased with that sport.

And because you that are but a young angler, know not what *snigling* is, I will now teach it to you : you remember I told you that *Eeles* do not usually stir in the day time, for then they hide themselves under some covert, or under boards, or planks about floud-gates, or weirs, or mils, or in holes in the river banks; and you observing your time in a warm day, when the water is lowest, may take a hook tied to a strong line, or to a string about a yard long, and then into one of these holes, or between any boards about a mill, or under any great stone or plank, or any place where you think an *Eele* may hide or shelter her selfe, there with the help of a short stick put in your bait, but leisurely, and as far as you may conveniently; and it is scarce to be doubted, but that if there be an *Eel* within the sight of it, the *Eele* will bite instantly, and as certainly gorge it; and you need not doubt to have him, if you pull him not out of the hole too quickly, but pull him out by degrees, for he lying folded double in his hole, will, with the help of his taile, break all, unless you give him time to be wearied with pulling, and so get him out by degrees; not pulling too hard. And thus much for this present time concerning the *Eele*: I wil next tel you a little of the *Barbell*, and hope with a little discourse of him, to have an end of this showr, and fal to fishing, for the weather clears up a little.

CHAP. XI.

Pisc. THE *Barbell,* is so called (sayes *Gesner*) from or by reason of his beard, or wattels at his mouth, his mouth being under his nose or chaps, and he is one of the leather mouthed fish that has his teeth in his throat, he loves to live in very swift streams, and where it is gravelly, and in the gravel will root or dig with his nose like a hog, and there nest himself, taking so fast hold of any weeds or moss that grows on stones, or on piles about *weirs,* or *floud-gates,* or *bridges,* that the water is not able, be it ever so swift, to force him from the place which he seems to contend for : this is his constant custome in summer, when both he, and most living creatures joy and sport themselves in the sun ; but at the approach of winter, then he forsakes the swift streams and shallow waters, and by degrees retires to those parts of the river that are quiet and deeper ; in which places, (and I think about that time) he spawns ; and as I have formerly told you, with the help of the melter, hides his spawn or eggs in holes, which they both dig in the gravel, and then they mutually labour to cover it with the same sand to prevent it from being devoured by other fish.

There be such store of this fish in the river *Danubie,* that Randelitius sayes, they may in some places of it, and in some months of the yeer, be taken by those that dwel neer to the river, with their hands, eight or ten load at a time ; he sayes, they begin to be good in *May,* and they cease to be so in *August ;* but it is found to be otherwise in this nation : but thus far we agree with him, that the spawne of a *Barbell* is, if it be not poison, as he sayes, yet that is dangerous meat, and especially in the month of *May ;* and *Gesner* declares, it had an ill effect upon him to the indangering of his life.

This fish is of a fine cast and handsome shape, and may be rather said not to be ill, than to bee good meat ; the *Chub* and he have (I think) both lost a part of their credit by ill cookery, they being reputed the worst or coarsest of fresh water fish : but the *Barbell* affords an *angler* choice sport, being a lustie and a cunning fish ; so lustie and cunning as to endanger the breaking of the anglers line, by running his head forcibly towards any covert or hole, or bank, and then striking at the line, to break it off with his tail (as is observed by *Plutarch*, in his book *de industria animalium*) and also so cunning to nibble and suck off your worme close to the hook, and yet avoid the letting the hook come into his mouth.

The *Barbell* is also curious for his baits, that is to say, that they be clean and sweet ; that is to say, to have your worms well scowred, and not kept in sowre or mustie moss ; [for at a well scowred lob-worm he will bite as boldly as at any bait, especially, if the night or two before you fish for him, you shall bait the places where you intend to fish for him with big worms cut into pieces : and gentles (not being too much scowred, but green) are a choice bait for him, and so is cheese, which is not to be too hard, but kept a day or two in a wet linnen cloth to make it tough ; with this you may also bait the water a day or two before you fish for the *Barbel*, and be much the likelier to catch store ; and if the cheese were laid in clarified honey a short time before (as namely, an hour or two) you were still the likelier to catch fish ; some have directed to cut the cheese into thin pieces, and toste it, and then tie it on the hook with fine silk : and some advise to fish for the *Barbell* with sheep's tallow and soft cheese beaten or work'd into a paste, and that it is choicely good in *August* ; and I believe it : but doubtless the lob-worm well scoured, and the gentle not too much scowred, and cheese ordered as I have directed, are baits enough, and I think will serve in any month ; though I shall commend any angler that tryes conclusions, and is industrious to improve the art. And now, my honest scholer, the long showre, and my tedious discourse are both ended together ; and I shall give you but this observation, that when you fish for a *Barbell*, your rod and line be both long, and of good strength, for you will find him a heavy and a doged fish to be dealt withal, yet he seldom or never breaks his hold if he be once strucken.

And now lets go and see what interest the *Trouts* will pay us for letting our *angle-rods* lye so long and quietly in the water. Come, scholer; which will you take up?

Viat. Which you think fit, master.

Pisc. Why, you shall take up that; for I am certain by viewing the line, it has a fish at it. Look you, scholer, well done. Come now, take up the other too; well, now you may tell my brother *Peter* at night, that you have caught a lease of *Trouts* this day. And now lets move toward our lodging, and drink a draught of *red cows milk*, as we go, and give pretty *Maudlin* and her mother a brace of *Trouts* for their supper.

Viat. Master, I like your motion very well, and I think it is now about milking time, and yonder they be at it.

Pisc. God speed you good woman, I thank you both for our songs last night; I and my companion had such fortune a fishing this day, that we resolve to give you and *Maudlin* a brace of *Trouts* for supper, and we will now taste a draught of your *red cows milk*.

Milkw. Marry, and that you shal with all my heart, and I will be still your debtor when you come next this way, if you will but speak the word, I will make you a good *sillabub*, and then you may sit down in a *hay-cock* and eat it, and *Maudlin* shal sit by you and sing you the good old Song of the *Hunting in Chevy Chase*, or some other good Ballad, for she hath good store of them: *Maudlin* hath a notable memory.

Viat. We thank you, and intend once in a month to call upon you again, and give you a little warning, and so good night; good night *Maudlin*. And now, good master, lets lose no time, but tell me somewhat more of fishing; and if you please, first something of fishing for a *Gudgion*.

Pisc. I will, honest scholer. The *Gudgion* is an excellent fish to eat, and good also to enter a young *angler;* he is easie to bee taken with a small red worm at the ground and is one of those leather mouthed fish that has his teeth in his throat, and will hardly be lost off from the hook if he be once strucken: they be usually scattered up and down every river in the shallows, in the heat of summer ; but in *autome*, when the weeds begin to grow sowre or rot, and the weather colder, then they gather together, and get into the deeper parts of the water, and are to be fish'd for there, with your hook alwaies touching the ground, if you fish for him with a flote or with a cork, but many will fish for the *Gudgion* by hand, with a running line upon the ground without a cork as a *Trout* is fished for, and it is an excellent way.

There is also another fish called a *Pope*, and by some a *Ruffe*, a fish that is not known to be in some rivers ; it is much like the *Pearch* for his shape, but will not grow to be bigger than a *Gudgion;* he is an excellent fish, no fish that swims is of a pleasanter taste ; and he is also excellent to enter a young *angler*, for he is a greedy biter, and they will usually lye abundance of them together in one reserved place where the water is deep, and runs quietly, and an easie angler, if he has found where they lye, may catch fortie or fiftie, or sometimes twice so many at a standing.

There is also a *Bleak*, a fish that is ever in motion, and therefore called by some the river swallow ; for just as you shall observe the *Swallow* to be most evenings in summer ever in motion, making short and quick turns when he flies to catch flies in the aire, by which he lives, so does the *Bleak* at the top of the water ; and this fish is best caught with a fine smal artificial fly, which is to be of a brown colour, and very smal, and the hook answerable : there is no better sport than whipping for *Bleaks* in a boat in a summers evening, with a hazle top about five or six foot long, and a line twice the length of the rod. I have heard Sir *Henry Wotton* say, that there be many that in *Italy* will catch *Swallows* so, or especially *Martins* (the bird-angler standing on the top of the steeple to do it, and with a line twice so long, as I have spoke of) and let me tell you, scholer, that both *Martins* and *Bleaks* be most excellent meat.

I might now tell you how to catch *Roch* and *Dace*, and some other fish of little note, that I have not yet spoke of ; but you see we are almost at our lodging, and indeed if we were not, I would omit to give you any directions concerning them, or how to fish for them, not but that they be both good fish (being in season) and especially to some palates, and they also make the angler good sport (and you know the hunter sayes, there is more sport in hunting the hare than in eating of her) but I will forbear to give any direction concerning them, because you may go a few dayes and take the pleasure of the fresh aire, and bear any common angler company that fishes for them, and by that means learn more than any direction I can give you in words, can make you capable of; and I will therefore end my discourse, for yonder comes our brother *Peter* and honest *Coridon*, but I will promise you that as you and I fish, and walk to morrow towards *London*, if I have now forgotten any thing, that I can then remember, I will not keep it from you.

Well met, gentlemen, this is luckie that we meet so just together at this very door. Come hostis, where are you? is supper ready? come, first give us drink, and be as quick as you can, for I believe wee are all very hungry. Wel, brother *Peter* and *Coridon* to you both; come drink, and tell me what luck of fish: we two have caught but ten *Trouts*, of which my scholer caught three; look here's eight, and a brace we gave away: we have had a most pleasant day for fishing, and talking, and now returned home both weary and hungry, and now meat and rest will be pleasant.

Pet. And *Coridon* and I have not had an unpleasant day, and yet I have caught but five *Trouts :* for indeed we went to a good honest ale-house, and there we plaid at shovel-board half the day; all the time that it rained we were there, and as merry as they that fish'd, and I am glad we are now with a dry house over our heads, for heark how it rains and blows. Come hostis, give us more ale, and our supper with what haste you may, and when we have sup'd, lets have your song *Piscator*, and the ketch that your scholer promised us, or else *Coridon* will be doged.

Pisc. Nay, I wil not be worse than my word, you shall not want my song, and I hope I shall be perfect in it.

Viat. And I hope the like for my ketch, which I have

ready too, and therefore lets go merrily to supper, and then have a gentle touch at singing and drinking ; but the last with moderation.

Cor. Come, now for your song, for we have fed heartily. Come hostis give us a little more drink, and lay a few more sticks on the fire, and now sing when you will.

Pisc. Well then, here's to you *Coridon;* and now for my song.

> Oh the brave fishers life,
> It is the best of any,
> 'Tis full of pleasure, void of strife
> And 'tis belov'd of many :
>> Other joyes
>> Are but toyes,
>> Only this
>> Lawful is,
>> For our skil
>> Breeds no ill,
> But content and pleasure.
>
> In a morning up we rise
> Ere *Aurora's* peeping,
> Drink a cup to wash our eyes,
> Leave the sluggard sleeping ;
>> Then we go
>> Too and fro,
>> With our knacks
>> At our backs,
>> To such streams
>> As the Thames
> If we have the leisure.
>
> When we please to walk abroad
> For our recreation,
> In the fields is our abode,
> Full of delectation :
>> Where in a brook
>> With a hook,
>> Or a lake
>> Fish we take,

There we sit
For a bit,
Till we fish intangle.

We have gentles in a horn,
We have paste and worms too,
We can watch both night and morn,
Suffer rain and storms too :
None do here
Use to swear,
Oathes do fray
Fish away,
We sit still,
Watch our quill,
Fishers must not rangle.

If the sun's excessive heat
Makes our bodies swelter,
To an osier hedge we get
For a friendly shelter,
Where in a dike
Perch or Pike
Roch or Dace
We do chase
Bleak or Gudgion
Without grudging,
We are still contented.

Or we sometimes pass an hour,
Under a green willow,
That defends us from a showr,
Making earth our pillow,
There we may
Think and pray
Before death
Stops our breath :
Other joyes
Are but toyes
And to be lamented.

Viat. Well sung, master; this dayes fortune and pleasure, and this nights company and song, do all make me

more and more in love with *angling.* Gentlemen, my
master left me alone for an hour this day, and I verily
believe he retir'd himself from talking with me, that he
might be so perfect in this song; was it not master?

Pisc. Yes indeed, for it is many yeers since I learn'd it,
and having forgotten a part of it, I was forced to patch it
up by the help of my own invention, who am not excellent
at poetry, as my part of the song may testifie: but of that
I will say no more, least you should think I mean by dis-
commending it, to beg your commendations of it. And
therefore without replications, lets hear your ketch, scholer,
which I hope will be a good one, for you are both musical,
and have a good fancie to boot.

Viat. Marry, and that you shall, and as freely as I
would have my honest master tel me some more secrets of
fish and fishing as we walk and fish towards *London* to
morrow. But master, first let me tell you, that that very
hour which you were absent from me, I sate down under
a willow tree by the water side, and considered what you
had told me of the owner of that pleasant meadow in
which you then left me, that he had a plentiful estate, and
not a heart to think so; that he had at this time many
law suites depending, and that they both damp'd his mirth
and took up so much of his time and thoughts, that he
himselfe had not leisure to take the sweet content that I,
who pretended no title, took in his fields; for I could there
sit quietly, and looking on the water, see fishes leaping at
flies of several shapes and colours; looking on the hils,
could behold them spotted with woods and groves: looking down the meadows, could see here a boy gathering
lillies and *lady-smocks,* and there a girle cropping *culver-
keys* and *cowslips,* all to make garlands suitable to this
pleasant month of May; these and many other field-
flowers so perfum'd the air, that I thought this meadow
like the field in Sicily (of which *Diodorus* speaks) where
the perfumes arising from the place, make all dogs that
hunt in it, to fall off, and to lose their hottest sent. I say,
as I thus sate joying in mine own happy condition, and
pittying that rich mans that ought this, and many other
pleasant groves and meadows about me, I did thankfully

remember what my Saviour said, that *the meek possess the earth ;* for indeed they are free from those high, those restless thoughts and contentions which corrode the sweets of life. For they, and they only, can say as the poet has happily exprest it,

> Hail blest estate of poverty !
> Happy enjoyment of such minds,
> As rich in low contentedness,
> Can, like the reeds in roughest winds,
>   By yielding make that blow but smal
>   At which proud oaks and cedars fal.

Gentlemen, these were a part of the thoughts that then possest me, and I there made a conversion of a piece of an old ketch, and added more to it, fitting them to be sung by us anglers : come master, you can sing well, you must sing a part of it as it is in this paper.

Pet. I marry sir, this is musick indeed, this has cheered my heart, and made me to remember six verses in praise of musick, which I will speak to you instantly.

> Musick, miraculous rhetorick, that speak'st sense
> Without a tongue, excelling eloquence ;
> With what ease might thy errors be excus'd
> Wert thou as truly lov'd as th'art abus'd,
> But though dull souls neglect, and some reprove thee
> I cannot hate thee, 'cause the angels love thee.

Piscat. Well remembred, brother *Peter*, these verses came seasonably. Come, we will all joine together, mine hoste and all, and sing my scholers ketch over again, and then each man drink the tother cup and to bed, and thank · God we have a dry house over our heads.

Pisc. Well now, good night to every body.

Pet. And so say I.

Viat. And so say I.

Cor. Good night to you all, and I thank you.

Pisc. Good morrow brother *Peter*, and the like to you, honest *Coridon ;* come, my hostis sayes there is seven shillings to pay, lets each man drink a pot for his mornings draught, and lay down his two shillings, that so my

hostess may not have occasion to repent herself of being
so diligent, and using us so kindly.

Pet. The motion is liked by every body ; and so hostis
here's your mony, we anglers are all beholding to you, it
wil not be long ere Ile see you again. And now brother
Piscator, I wish you and my brother your scholer a fair
day, and good fortune.   Come *Coridon*, this is our way.

CHAP XII.

Viat. GOOD master, as we go now towards *London*, be
still so courteous as to give me more instructions, for I
have several boxes in my memory in which I will keep
them all very safe, there shall not one of them be lost.

Pisc. Well scholer, that I will, and I will hide nothing
from you that I can remember, and may help you forward
towards a perfection in this art ; and because we have so
much time, and I have said so little of *Roch* and *Dace*,
I will give you some directions concerning some several
kinds of baits with which they be usually taken ; they will
bite almost at any flies, but especially at ant-flies ; concerning which, take this direction, for it is very good.

Take the blackish *ant-fly* out of the mole-hill, or ant-hil,
in which place you shall find them in the months of June ;
or if that be too early in the yeer, then doubtless you may
find them in *July*, *August*, and most of September ;
gather them alive with both their wings, and then put
them into a glass, that will hold a quart or a pottle ; but
first, put into the glass, a handful or more of the moist
earth out of which you gather them, and as much of the
roots of the grass of the said hillock ; and then put in the
flies gently, that they lose not their wings, and so many as
are put into the glass without bruising, will live there a
month or more, and be alwaies in a readiness for you to
fish with ; but if you would have them keep longer, then
get any great earthern pot or barrel of three or four gallons
(which is better) then wash your barrel with water and
honey ; and having put into it a quantitie of earth and

grass roots, then put in your flies and cover it, and they
will live a quarter of a year; these in any stream and
clear water are a deadly bait for *Rock* or *Dace*, or for a
Chub, and your rule is to fish not less than a handful from
the bottom.

I shall next tell you a winter bait for a *Rock*, a *Dace*, or
Chub, and it is choicely good. About *all-hallantide* (and
so till frost comes) when you see men ploughing up heath-
ground, or sandy-ground, or greenswards, then follow the
plough, and you shall find a white worm, as big as two
magots, and it hath a red head, (you may observe in what
ground most are, for there the crows will be very watchful,
and follow the plough very close) it is all soft, and full of
whitish guts; a worm that is in Norfolk and some other
countries called a *Grub*, and is bred of the spawn or eggs
of a beetle, which she leaves in holes that she digs in the
ground under cow or horse-dung, and there rests all winter, and in March or April comes to be first a red, and
then a black beetle: gather a thousand or two of these,
and put them with a peck or two of their own earth into
some tub or firkin, and cover and keep them so warm,
that the frost or cold air, or winds kill them not, and you
may keep them all winter and kill fish with them at any
time, and if you put some of them into a little earth and
honey a day before you use them, you will find them an
excellent bait for *Breame* or *Carp*.

And after this manner you may also keep gentles all
winter, which is a good bait then, and much the better for
being lively and tuffe, or you may breed and keep gentles
thus: take a piece of beasts liver and with a cross stick,
hang it in some corner over a pot or barrel half full of dry
clay, and as the gentles grow big, they wil fall into the
barrel and scowre themselves, and be alwayes ready for
use whensoever you incline to fish; and these gentles may
be thus made til after Michaelmas: but if you desire to
keep gentles to fish with all the yeer, then get a dead *cat*
or a *kite*, and let it be fly-blowne, and when the gentles
begin to be alive and to stir then bury it and them in
moist earth, but as free from frost as you can, and these
you may dig up at any time when you intend to use them;

these will last till *March*, and about that time turn to be flies.

But if you be nice to fowl your fingers (which good anglers seldome are) then take this bait : get a handful of well made mault, and put it into a dish of water, and then wash and rub it betwixt your hands till you make it cleane, and as free from husks as you can ; then put that water from it, and put a smal quantitie of fresh water to it, and set it in something that is fit for that purpose, over the fire, where it is not to boil apace, but leisurely, and very softly, until it become somewhat soft, which you may try by feeling it betwixt your finger and thumb ; and when it is soft, then put your water from it, and then take a sharp knife, and turning the sprout end of the corn upward, with the point of your knife take the back part of the husk off from it, and yet leaving a kind of husk on the corn, or else it is marr'd ; and then cut off that sprouted end (I mean a little of it) that the white may appear, and so pull off the husk on the cloven side (as I directed you) and then cutting off a very little of the other end, that so your hook may enter, and if your hook be small and good, you will find this to be a very choice bait either for winter or summer, you sometimes casting a little of it into the place where your flote swims.

And to take the *Roch* and *Dace*, a good bait is the young brood of wasps or bees, baked or hardned in their husks in an oven, after the bread is taken out of it, or on a fire-shovel ; and so also is the thick blood of *sheep*, beinge halfe dried on a trencher that you may cut it into such pieces as may best fit the size of your hook, and a little salt keeps it from growing black, and makes it not the worse but better ; this is taken to be a choice bait, if rightly ordered.

There be several oiles of a strong smel that I have been told of, and be excellent to tempt fish to bite, of which I could say much, but I remember I once carried a small bottle from sir *George Hastings* to sir *Henry Wotton* (they were both chimical men) as a great present ; but upon enquiry, I found it did not answer the expectation of sir *Henry*, which with the help of other circumstances, makes

7

me have little belief in such things as many men talk of;
not but that I think fishes both smell and hear (as I have
exprest in my former discourse) but there is a mysterious
knack, which (though it be much easier than the philoso-
phers-stone, yet) is not atainable by common capacities,
or else lies locked up in the braine or brest of some chimical men, that, like the *Rosi-crutions*, yet will not reveal it.
But I stepped by chance into this discourse of oiles, and
fishes smelling ; and though there might be more said,
both of it, and of baits for *Roch* and *Dace*, and other flote
fish, yet I will forbear it at this time, and tell you in the
next place how you are to prepare your tackling : concerning which I will for sport sake give you an old rhime
out of an old fish-book, which will be a part of what you
are to provide.

My rod, and my line, my flote and my lead,
My hook, and my plummet, my whetstone and knife,
My basket, my baits, both living and dead,
My net, and my meat, for that is the chief ;
Then I must have thred and hairs great and smal,
With mine angling purse, and so you have all.

But you must have all these tackling, and twice so many
more, with which, if you mean to be a fisher, you must
store your selfe : and to that purpose I will go with you
either to *Charles Brandons* (neer to the *Swan* in *Golding-
lane*); or to Mr. *Fletchers* in the Court which did once
belong to Dr. *Nowel* the Dean of *Pauls*, that I told you
was a good man, and a good fisher; it is hard by the west
end of Saint *Pauls* church ; they be both honest men, and
will fit an angler with what tackling hee wants.

Viat. Then, good master, let it be at *Charles Brandons*,
for he is neerest to my dwelling, and I pray lets meet
there the ninth of *May* next about two of the clock,
and I'l want nothing that a fisher should be furnish'd with.

Pisc. Well, and Ile not fail you, God willing, at the time
and place appointed.

Viat. I thank you, good master, and I will not fail you :
and good master, tell me what baits more you remember,
for it wil not now be long ere we shal be at *Totenham*

High-Cross, and when we come thither, I wil make you some requital of your pains, by repeating as choice a copy of verses, as any we have heard since we met together, and that is a proud word ; for wee have heard very good ones.

Pisc. Wel, scholer, and I shal be right glad to hear them ; and I will tel you whatsoever comes in my mind, that I think may be worth your hearing : you may make another choice bait thus, take a hand ful or two of the best and biggest *wheat* you can get, boil it in a little milk like as frumitie is boiled, boil it so till it be soft, and then fry it very leisurely with honey, and a little beaten *saffron* dissolved in milk, and you wil find this a choice bait, and good I think for any fish, especially for *Roch*, *Dace*, *Chub* or *Greyling ;* I know not but that it may be as good for a river *Carp*, and especially if the ground be a little baited with it.

You are also to know, that there be divers kinds of *cadis*, or *case-worms*, that are to bee found in this nation in several distinct counties, and in several little brooks that relate to bigger rivers, as namely one *cadis* called a *piper*, whose husk or case is a piece of reed about an inch long or longer, and as big about as the compass of a two pence ; these worms being kept three or four days in a woollen bag with sand at the bottom of it, and the bag wet once a day, will in three or four dayes turne to be yellow ; and these be a choice bait for the *Chub* or *Chavender*, or indeed for any great fish, for it is a large bait.

There is also a lesser *cadis-worm*, called a *cock-spur*, being in fashion like the spur of a cock, sharp at one end, and the case or house in which this dwels is made of smal *husks* and *gravel*, and *slime*, most curiously made of these, even so as to be wondred at, but not made by man (no more than the nest of a bird is :) this is a choice bait for any flote fish, it is much less than the *piper cadis*, and to be so ordered ; and these may be so preserved ten, fifteen, or twentie dayes.

There is also another *cadis* called by some a *straw-worm*, and by some a *ruffe-coate*, whose house or case is made of little pieces of bents, and rushes, and straws, and

7—2

water weeds, and I know not what, which are so knit together with condens'd slime, that they stick up about her husk or case, not unlike the bristles of a *hedg-hog;* these three *cadis* are commonly taken in the beginning of summer, and are good indeed to take any kind of fish with flote or otherwise. I might tell of you many more, which, as these doe early, so those have their time of turning to be flies later in summer; but I might lose my selfe, and tire you by such a discourse, I shall therefore but remember you, that to know these, and their several kinds, and to what flies every particular *cadis* turns, and then how use them, first as they bee *cadis,* and then as they be flies, is an art, and an art that every one that professes angling is not capable of.

But let mee tell you, I have been much pleased to walk quietly by a brook with a little stick in my hand, with which I might easily take these, and consider the curiosity of their composure; and if you shall ever like to do so, then note, that your stick must be cleft, or have a nick at one end of it, by which meanes you may with ease take many of them of the water, before you have any occasion to use them. These, my honest scholer, are some observations told to you as they now come suddenly into my memory, of which you may make some use : but for the practical part, it is that that makes an angler; it is diligence, and observation, and practice that must do it.

CHAP. XIII.

Pisc. WELL, scholer, I have held you too long about these *cadis,* and my spirits are almost spent, and so I doubt is your patience; but being we are now within sight of *Totenham,* where I first met you, and where wee are to part, I will give you a little direction how to colour the hair of which you make your lines, for that is very needful to be known of an *angler;* and also how to paint your rod, especially your top, for a right grown top is a choice commoditie, and should be preserved from the water soking into it, which makes it in wet weather to be heavy, and fish ill favouredly, and also to rot quickly.

Take a pint of strong ale, half a pound of soot, and a like quantity of the juice of walnut-tree leaves, and an equal quantitie of allome, put these together into a pot, or pan, or pipkin, and boil them half an hour, and having so done, let it cool, and being cold, put your hair into it, and there let it lye ; it wil turn your hair to be a kind of water, or glass colour, or greenish ; and the longer you let it lye, the deeper coloured it will bee ; you might be taught to make many other colours, but it is to little purpose ; for doubtlesse the water or glass coloured haire is the most choice and most useful for an *angler*.

But if you desire to colour haire green, then doe it thus : take a quart of smal ale, half a pound of allome, then put these into a pan or pipkin, and your haire into it with them, then put it upon a fire and let it boile softly for half an hour, and then take out your hair, and let it dry, and having so done, then take a pottle of water, and put into it two handful of mary-golds, and cover it with a tile or what you think fit, and set it again on the fire, where it is to boil softly for half an hour, about which time the scum will turn yellow, then put into it half a pound of copporis beaten smal, and with it the hair that you intend to colour, then let the hair be boiled softly till half the liquor be wasted, and then let it cool three or four hours with your hair in it ; and you are to observe, that the more copporis you put into it, the greener it will be, but doubtless the pale green is best ; but if you desire yellow hair (which is only good when the weeds rot) then put in the more *mary-golds*, and abate most of the *copporis*, or leave it out, and take a little verdigreece in stead of it.

This for colouring your hair. And as for painting your rod, which must be in oyl, you must first make a size with glue and water, boiled together until the glue be dissolved, and the size of a lie colour ; then strike your size upon the wood with a bristle brush or pensil, whilst it is hot : that being quite dry, take white lead, and a little red lead, and a little cole black, so much as all together will make

an ash colour, grind these all together with linseed oyle,
let it be thick, and lay it then upon the wood with a brush
or pensil, this do for the ground of any colour to lie upon
wood.

For a Green.

Take pink and verdigreece, and grind them together in
linseed oyl, as thick as you can well grind, then lay it
smoothly on with your brush, and drive it thin, once doing
for the most part will serve, if you lay it wel, and be sure
your first colour be thoroughly dry, before you lay on a
second.

Well, scholer, you now see *Totenham*, and I am weary,
and therefore glad that we are so near it; but if I were to
walk many more dayes with you, I could stil be telling
you more and more of the mysterious art of angling; but
I wil hope for another opportunitie, and then I wil acquaint
you with many more, both necessary and true observations
concerning fish and fishing : but now no more, lets turn
into yonder arbour, for it is a cleane and cool place.

Viat. 'Tis a faire motion, and I will requite a part of
your courtesies with a bottle of *sack*, and milk and *oranges*
and *sugar*, which all put together, make a drink too good
for any body but us anglers : and so master, here is a full
glass to you of that liquor, and when you have pledged
me, I will repeat the verses which I promised you, it is a
copy printed amongst Sir *Henry Wotton's* verses, and
doubtless made either by him, or by a lover of angling :
come master, now drink a glass to me, and then I will
pledge you, and fall to my repetition ; it is a description of
such country recreations as I have enjoyed since I had the
happiness to fall into your company.

> Quivering fears, heart tearing cares,
> Anxious sighes, untimely tears,
>   Fly, fly to courts,
>   Fly to fond worldlings sports,
> Where strain'd sardonick smiles are glosing still
> And grief is forc'd to laugh against her will.
>   Where mirths but mummery,
>   And sorrows only real be.

Fly from our country pastimes, fly,
Sad troops of humane misery,
  Come serene looks,
  Clear as the christal brooks,
Or the pure azur'd heaven that smiles to see
The rich attendance on our poverty ;
  Peace and a secure mind
  Which all men seek we only find.

Abused mortals did you know
Where joy, hearts ease, and comforts grow,
  You'd scorn proud towers,
  And seek them in these bowers,
Where winds sometimes our woods perhaps may shake,
But blustering care could never tempest make,
  No murmurs ere come nigh us,
  Saving of fountains that glide by us.

Here's no fantastick mask nor dance,
But of our kids that frisk and prance ;
  Nor wars are seen
  Unless upon the green
Two harmless lambs are butting one the other,
Which done, both bleating, run each to his mother :
  And wounds are never found,
Save what the plough-share gives the ground.

Here are no false entrapping baits
To hasten too too hasty fates ;
  Unless it be
  The fond credulitie
Of silly fish, which, worldling like, still look
Upon the bait, but never on the hook ;
  Nor envy, 'nless among
  The birds, for price of their sweet song.

Go, let the diving *Negro* seek
For gems hid in some forlorn creek,
  We all pearls scorn,
  Save what the dewy morne
Congeals upon each little spire of grasse,
Which careless shepherds beat down as they passe,

And gold ne'er here appears
Save what the yellow *Ceres* bears.

Blest silent groves, oh may you be
For ever mirths best nursery,
 May pure contents
 For ever pitch their tents
Upon these downs, these meads, these rocks, these moun-
  tains,
And peace stil slumber by these purling fountains
 Which we may every year
 Find when we come a fishing here.

Pisc. Trust me, scholer, I thank you heartily for these
verses, they be choicely good, and doubtless made by a
lover of angling : come, now drink a glass to me, and I
will requite you with a very good copy of verses ; it is a
farewel to the vanities of the world, and some say written
by *D*ʳ. *D.*, but let them bee writ by whom they will, he
that writ them had a brave soul, and must needs be possest with happy thoughts at the time of their composure.

Farwel ye guilded follies, pleasing troubles.
Farwel ye honour'd rags, ye glorious bubbles,
Fame's but a hollow eccho, gold pure clay,
Honour the darling but of one short day.
Beauty (th' eyes idol) but a damask'd skin,
State but a golden prison, to live in
And torture free-born minds ; imbroider'd trains
Meerly but pageants, for proud swelling vains,
And blood ally'd to greatness, is alone
Inherited, not purchas'd, nor our own.
 Fame, honor, beauty, state, train, blood and birth,
 Are but the fading blossomes of the earth.

I would be great, but that the sun doth still,
Level his rayes against the rising hill :
I would be high, but see the proudest oak
Most subject to the rending thunder-stroke ;
I would be rich, but see men too unkind
Dig in the bowels of the richest mind ;

I would be wise, but that I often see
The fox suspected whilst the ass goes free ;
I would be fair, but see the fair and proud
Like the bright sun, oft setting in a cloud ;
I would be poor, but know the humble grass
Still trampled on by each unworthy asse :
Rich, hated ; wise, suspected ; scorn'd, if poor ;
Great, fear'd ; fair, tempted ; high, stil envi'd more
   I have wish'd all, but now I wish for neither,
   Great, high, rich, wise, nor fair, poor I'l be rather.

Would the world now adopt me for her heir,
Would beauties queen entitle me the fair,
Fame speak me fortunes minion, could I vie
Angels wth *India*, wth a speaking eye
Command bare heads, bow'd knees strike justice dumb
As well as blind and lame, or give a tongue
To stones, by epitaphs, be call'd great master
In the loose rhimes of every poetaster ;
Could I be more than any man that lives,
Great, fair, rich, wise in all superlatives ;
Yet I more freely would these gifts resign,
Than ever fortune would have made them mine ;
   And hold one minute of this holy leasure
   Beyond the riches of this empty pleasure.

Welcom pure thoughts, welcome ye silent groves,
These guests, these courts, my soul most dearly loves,
Now the wing'd people of the skie shall sing
My cheerful anthems to the gladsome spring ;
A pray'r book now shall be my looking glasse,
In which I will adore sweet vertues face.
Here dwell no hateful looks, no pallace cares,
No broken vows dwell here, nor pale fac'd fears,
Then here I'l sit and sigh my hot loves folly,
And learn t'affect an holy melancholy.
   And if contentment be a stranger, then
   I'l nere look for it, but in heaven again.

Viat. Wel master, these be verses that be worthy to
keep a room in every mans memory. I thank you for

them, and I thank you for your many instructions, which I will not forget ; your company and discourse have been so pleasant, that I may truly say, I have only lived, since I enjoyed you and them, and turned angler. I am sorry tq part with you here, here in this place where I first met you, but it must be so : I shall long for the ninth of *May,* for then we are to meet at *Charles Brandons.* This intermitted time wil seem to me (as it does to men in sorrow) to pass slowly, but I wil hasten it as fast as *I* can by my wishes, and in the mean time *the blessing of Saint Peters Master be with mine.*

Pisc. And the like be upon my honest scholar. And upon all that hate contentions, and love *quietnesse,* and *vertue,* and *Angling.*

BIBLIOGRAPHY OF THIS WORK.

1. London, 1653, 12mo., *of which this is a reprint.*		
2. ,, 1655, 16mo.	20. London, 1833-6, imp. 8vo.
3. ,, 1661, ,,	21. ,, 1835, fcap. 8vo.
4. ,, 1664, ,,	22. ,, 1837, 24mo.
5. ,, 1668, ,,	23. ,, 1839, 12mo.
6. ,, 1676, ,,	24. ,, 1839, fcap. 8vo.
7. ,, 1676, 12mo.	25. ,, 1842, ,, ,,
8. ,, 1750, ,,	26. ,, 1844, ,, ,,
9. ,, 1760, 8vo.	27. New York, 1847, 8vo.
10. ,, 1806, ,,	28. Manchester, 1851, 12mo.
11. ,, 1810, 16mo.	29. London, 1851, 12mo.
12. ,, 1822, 8vo.	30. ,, 1853, post 8vo.
13. ,, 1823, fcap. 8vo.	31. ,, 1856, ,, ,,
14. ,, 1824, ,, ,,	32. ,, 1858, 24mo.
15. ,, 1824, 24mo.	33. ,, 1859, post 8vo.
16. ,, 1825, 18mo.	34. ,, 1863, ,, ,,
17. ,, 1825, 48mo.	35. ,, 1869, crown 8vo.
18. ,, 1826, 24mo.	[*this edition.*
19. ,, 1826, 32mo.	LOWNDES.

May. A. M

FINIS.

Billing, Printer, Guildford.

May, 1869.

REPRINTS EDITED BY A. MURRAY.

CROWN 8VO., TONED PAPER, CLOTH LETTERED, &C.

Gibbon's Autobiography and Correspondence.

One volume, 356 pp. Price 3s. 6d.
A REPRINT of the SHEFFIELD 4TO. EDITION, 1796.

Decline and Fall of the Roman Empire.

Complete in 3 volumes, 2,400 pp. Price 18s.
A REPRINT of the ORIGINAL 12-VOL. 8VO. EDITION, 1796, containing TEXT and NOTES, and only the words of Edward Gibbon.

History of the Crusades, By E. GIBBON.

132 pp. Cloth Limp, Red Edges, 1s.

Rise and Fall of the Saracen Empire.

By E. GIBBON.
146 pp. Cloth Limp, Red Edges, 1s.

Hallam's Europe during the Middle Ages.

In 1 volume. A careful REPRINT (TEXT and NOTES) of the FOURTH EDITION. Library Edition, 9s.; Cheap Edition, 6s.; People's Edition, 4s. Or in 2 vols.: I. History; II. Church and State; 2s. 6d. each.

Montaigne; All the Essays of Michel Signeur de.

1 vol., 916 pp., 7s. 6d., or bevelled boards, gilt edges, 8s. 6d.
A REPRINT of the COTTON TRANSLATION of 1700, collated with that of PETER COSTE.

Scott's Minstrelsy of the Scottish Border.

1 vol., 544 pp., 3s. 6d., or bevelled boards, gilt edges, 4s.
A REPRINT of the ORIGINAL EDITION, with ADDITIONAL MATTER.

Walton's Compleat Angler.

112 pp. Cloth limp, 1s.
REPRINTED FROM THE FIRST EDITION.

⁎ Above works are unique as to price and care of production, and challenge comparison with the best of the preceding editions.

London: A. MURRAY & SON, 30, Queen Square, W.C.

9 781017 142259